THE
CENTER WITHIN

THE
CENTER WITHIN

Gyomay M. Kubose

Dharma House Publishing
Bright Dawn Center of Oneness Buddhism
28372 Margaret Road
Coarsegold, CA 93614
www.brightdawn.org
brightdawn@kubose.com

Fourth printing 2015

Printed in the United States of America

ISBN # 978-0-9642-9924-5

*To my wife, Minnie,
without whose concern and
help, I could not have
come this far.*

FOREWORD

In our utilitarian and pragmatic culture the value of things and activities is based on the results they produce. Anything that does not bring good results or profit has no value. In this pecuniary society, unless an endeavor produces a good profit, it is a waste of time and energy.

Once I was invited to the annual dinner of a certain community organization. I was seated at a table with several other people. One person who was a member of the organization said to a young man at the table, "You are not a member; you should join the organization." The young man asked, "What is the membership fee?" When told "It's only 15 dollars a year," he replied, "$15 a year? What do I get?" The member said, "You shouldn't talk like that. Just pay the dues and work hard for the good of other people. There are many unfortunate people in this world."

I thought it was an interesting conversation. There are many people who think just for themselves. They are totally indifferent to others. If people thought more about others, this world would be a better place to live. It is because humans can develop a sense of universal goodness that they can be considered better than other animals.

Each individual person has something unique to himself. He has a capacity to develop his uniqueness. Particularly in this democratic society, he has the opportunity to develop his potential. Therefore, it is important for each individual to look within and find oneself and be oneself. This is an important teaching and philosophy of life. Everybody cannot be an outstanding musician or engineer. Everybody cannot be a general; foot soldiers are equally important. A janitor is important, as well as the president of a company. A piano is nice in the center of the living room, and a wastebasket is important in the corner. A door mat is doing an important job, although everyone steps on it. Everything has its place in this world. Each of us should look within and find one's own center and develop oneself to the fullest capacity. Everything has its center. A nation has its center; a family has its center. Each individual has a center around which his whole life revolves. It is of prime importance to find this center within one's own life. There are many people who are unable to find the center of their lives and consequently become frustrated and unhappy.

The articles in this book were transcribed from talks given over the years. Their original form has been preserved as much as possible and are expressions from my everyday life. If these articles help readers to find their centers and live fulfilling and meaningful lives, the purpose of the book is fulfilled.

Gyomay Masao Kubose
Chicago
Spring of 1986

TABLE OF CONTENTS

TABLE OF CONTENTS

AWARENESS

Buddhism is awareness. In our lives, unless we are aware, we will not see the truth: the truth about ourselves, other things, and the truth about other lives.

It is our tendency to always look outside—around us. We forget to look deep within. When we practice self-introspection, we can see all kinds of things. Yes, we have capabilities and virtues. But also our ego is strong and we have many ugly things within us. When we are serene and quiet we are able to see much deeper into all things.

All around us are many wonderful, beautiful things. Basho, the most famous of all Japanese poets, wrote many poems which were expressions of his life. He saw universal life—the pure life—deeply within himself and in all things around him. One of his well-known poems is:

yoku mire ba	Look carefully.
nazuna hana saku	The nazuna blooms
kaki ne kana	Along the fence—Ah!

The *nazuna* is a most insignificant, small flower. Unless one looks very carefully, one will not see it. Unless one understands life deeply, what significance can the *nazuna* have? Wild flowers bloom everywhere. What of them? Perhaps Basho had walked along that fence many times and had been totally unaware of that small, white flower until he saw it that particular morning. It was blooming with every petal, every leaf.

How beautiful! When the sun comes, the *nazuna* opens up one hundred percent. How about me? Am I living like the *nazuna*? I have so many complaints—no inspiration. But look at this small, insignificant wild flower. No one looks at it; no one praises it. However, it lives fully. Basho was inspired to live like the *nazuna* and crystallized his understanding into a 17-syllable haiku poem. Basho received a great lesson from the *nazuna* and this expanded his awareness.

Unless we are aware, we do not learn anything. We have no inspiration and no teachings. Teachings are everywhere—all around us—if only we open the mind's eye to see. Awareness of life is what makes life special. To learn Buddhism is to change one's life. Regardless of how much we learn, unless your life changes, nothing is learned—it is just accumulated knowledge. Without awareness, it is just another day and another place. To learn Buddhism is to become aware of life, which means to become aware of oneself.

A SHINING STAR

Here is a question: "Suppose you meet an enlightened person, what would you do? He knows everything. Explanation is not needed, and yet you should not be silent. How would you act?"

Well, you meet enlightened ones every day. As soon as you step out the door you meet birds, dogs, flowers, the sky. Enlightenment is something beyond speech and silence. Meet each thing face to face. This is important. A flower blooms, a dog barks, the wind blows. We have to be aware.

On December 8th, Bodhi Day, Siddartha met the morning star—gently, kindly, and he attained enlightenment. Siddartha had seen the stars many times, but that particular morning he met the morning star face to face. The star was shining. When Siddartha met that shining star he understood, and a new life was started.

Do not over-intellectualize. Enlightenment does not need intellectualization. In life, there is immediate touch, immediate communication—a spark between lives. Beyond speech and silence there is a true world. This is the world that all true Buddhists have experienced for themselves and revealed to others. The whole world is enlightened. You are in enlightenment. Just open your life and meet it directly, intimately. For this you need awareness. You try to find enlightenment elsewhere but it is here in your everyday life. The star is here, and shining.

BUDDHA NATURE AND GASSHO

Everyone has Buddha nature, the potential to become a Buddha. Because of this we treat all with highest respect and greet them with gassho, a bow. I think this is a wonderful teaching—to respect others. If you tell a small child, "You are a rascal," he will have no sense of self-respect. However, if you assure him of his goodness he will respect himself and become good. In the same way we gassho and remind each other that we are potentially Buddhas. This creates an atmosphere of honor and respect and we cannot help but respond accordingly.

Someone might say, "Well, even if you respect those drunkards lying around on the street, they don't know it." Even so, if you look down on them, abuse them, what good is that? Perhaps none were drunkards as young adults. Perhaps they all tried to be different. Due to circumstances of human weaknesses, they lost the way of their true lives, despaired, became angry—whatever the reasons, they became the way they are. We should understand such persons rather than look down on them. We must respect other people in order to create a better atmosphere; respect helps create peace in the world.

When my teacher became head of the Higashi Honganji Temple, he made the following motto for that particular year: World Peace Begins with Gassho. The more I thought about this, the truer it became for me. Peace in the home begins with gassho, too. Gassho is not necessarily shown only by its form—the putting together of the hands and bowing. Without the form there is still gassho. Gassho begins in each individual's mind—the mind where we are able to respect others. When a husband respects his wife and vice versa and when parents respect children and vice versa, there is the foundation for peace. Virtue is not our own; virtue always has neighbors. This is how the attitude of gassho can start to vibrate in our environment. It is through gassho that we can fulfill the Buddha nature within us.

BUDDHISM IS EVERYDAY LIFE

When Nansen, a teacher, was asked, "What is Buddhism?" he answered, "Everyday life." This is one of the many ways to point out the essence of Buddhism. In Buddhism we talk about the "way" or "path." In Chinese it is called "Tao," in Japanese, "Do." "Do" is the path or the way we live each day. What is this path? What kind of path do you walk? We make many pretensions, and we represent things as we want them to be. We do not see things as they are. We do not understand life "as it is." Buddhism is the most natural way of life where every little thing we do is *the way*.

Without pretensions or artificiality, each path is uniquely an individual's own. Each way is different and yet there is the Great Way that everyone walks. It is the same path but different to each individual. It can be difficult to understand that the universal Way is one's own way. This is the difference between the true way and the not-true way. Just as freedom is different from lawlessness, freedom is always one with law. Freedom exists when law is lived. What this means is that one must find the way deep inside oneself. Yet at the same time the way does exist "out there." Outside and inside become identical. The universal and particular become one. You live your own life and there is no pre-established pattern. Yet your unique pattern forms the same way the universe forms. This is life's path. It is a flower blooming, the wind blowing. You live; I live.

When you live the universal Way, you see life expressing itself everywhere. It is such a tremendous, noble life that you cannot help being inspired. Life is art when lived this way. Art means it is absolute. There is creativity in life; imitation has no value. Art must be original and unique. The art of haiku, Japanese poetry, is the Buddhist life expressed in poetic form. Each moment in life is a poem in itself. When each action is an expression of life itself there is beauty and fulfillment. This is the universal path. It is the way that Nansen pointed to, when he said, "Buddhism is everyday life."

EMPTY-HANDED

In Buddhism it is said, "Go with empty hands." To go empty-handed means to have no fixed ideas, no rigid plans. It means to be ever-ready; whatever comes we will receive it one hundred percent, do it one hundred percent.

Suppose you bring beautiful flowers or a box of candy to a friend. Some might say that taking something with you is not going empty-handed. However, empty-handed does not mean nothing in the hands; it is a condition of the mind. You simply want to give flowers out of real joy. There is no idea of "I am giving; I will be thanked, or I am returning a favor." There are no expectations. This is empty-handedness. Life as it is, without speculation, without intention.

Emptiness or nothingness means that there is no manipulation and no planning by the you, which is the accumulation of your five senses. Both sides of the struggle: I want to, I don't want to, must be forgotten. So it is said, where there is enlightenment, there is no self. Where there is self, there is no enlightenment. Both self and non-self must disappear. When non-self is conceptualized as non-self, then it is not non-self. Many people become attached to the idea of non-self and to the idea of nothingness. But when we are attached to nothingness, this kind of nothingness is not what Buddhism teaches. True nothingness is to be fully aware.

In the fresh, creative life there are no rigid plans. But some people say, "Don't we have to plan for tomorrow, for next year?" Yes, we make plans, but they should only be tentative guidelines. To have "no plan" means that when you actually do something you put your whole life into it, whatever it is. The minute we say, "I must be selfless," then that is fixed, not free. Go at it with your total self. Let life take over. When we really do things the self is transcended. In that kind of life every moment is fresh. Every minute is creative. This is what empty-handed means.

LAUGHTER

Buddhism teaches us how to laugh about life. Laughter is the basis of a healthy life. This laughter is hearty, total, and from the abdomen. To smile is easy. It is only the surface of life—above the neck. But to laugh! I remember the editor of one of the religious newspapers in Japan. This man really could laugh. If you had a problem, you didn't need counseling or advice. Just being with him and hearing him laugh dissolved the whole problem. Where did this healthy laugh come from? It came from a true understanding of life.

This laughter is not laughter for fun. The laughter that Buddhism points to is larger in scope and deeper in dimension. People who become tense, melancholy, and have nervous breakdowns—they cannot laugh. They are so involved in "serious" things. But the reality of life is impermanence. The Buddha taught that life is continuous change. Everything does change, good things, bad things, pleasant things, and unpleasant things—all are constantly flowing. All things are in the great current of life, and here is a little man trying to keep something and attach himself to something, thus creating misery. When one sees how small he is, what a fool he is, a little man trying to stem the whole tide of the universe—he then is able to laugh.

Let's learn to laugh. We are too serious about little things. We forget the larger perspective. We become attached to things—a particular business, a particular person. We worry so much about it. We are quite foolish beings. Attached to non-attachable things. Even when we understand non-attachment, we become attached to the idea of non-attachment. By depending upon undependable things we create our own problems. They seem big and we become frustrated. If we can laugh at our little mistakes and then extend that and laugh at our own basic ignorance—a big laugh, then this makes for a healthy life.

RHYTHM IN LIFE

Fatigue comes into your daily life because there are too many things in your mind. If you are able to do one thing at a time, it would be a wonderful way of life. One thing after another, in sequence—and when you do it, really do it. When it is finished forget about it. There must be a vacant space or time, an emptiness, between one thing and another. This vacant time is really relaxing. If you are continually on the go, continually tense, then you will quickly get tired. Life is like a series of waves. There is a certain rhythm. This rhythm is important and you should be one with it.

When you experience Buddhism you start to live a concentrated life. This concentration goes beyond simple concentration; it is a selfless concentration where the real self emerges. It is like a runner preparing for a hundred-yard dash. When the starter says, "On your mark, get set . . ." the entire body from the top of his head to the tip of his toes—his whole life—is all prepared to go. It is the most tense moment. When the pistol goes off—dash! There are no other thoughts. His whole life goes out to accomplish the hundred-yard dash. When the race is finished, it is finished. Forget about it.

In the course of life we have to plan. We consider every possible point and make our plan. However, once the plan is set, we execute and carry it out. We should do one thing at a time and do it whole-heartedly. Then, we should move on to the next thing. Buddhism teaches us this attitude. It is this kind of rhythm in life we have to learn.

TOKUSAN'S CANDLE

Tokusan was a great scholar of Buddhism. However, being a sincere seeker, he came to see that he hadn't realized the truth of Buddhism. During his travels he was directed to Ryutan, a Buddhist teacher. Tokusan met with Ryutan and asked many questions. Tokusan was amazed that there was so much to be learned that was not in books. Their discussion lasted late into the night. It was pitch dark when Tokusan started to leave. He was in a strange part of the country so he returned to Ryutan's study and said, "It is dark and there is no moon." "Oh," said Ryutan, "You had better take a light with you." So Ryutan lit a candle and handed it to Tokusan. As Tokusan was about to step outside, Ryutan blew the candle out! At that moment Tokusan's mind was opened; he understood. The next day he burned all his scholarly notes and commentaries.

In this story, what did Tokusan understand? Tokusan was a great scholar of Buddhism; he knew the teachings, all the terminology, thoughts and ideas. He possessed them as though they were his, but they were external things. They were not his, instead he belonged to them! One cannot depend upon external things. If one's peace or happiness depends upon external things, then that kind of peace or happiness is fragile and cannot be trusted. You have to find out in your own life what Tokusan found. In our everyday life we depend on external things: money, friends, good health, reputation. Most of our peace and happiness is based on such external things. Then, when life hits us hard we find nothing to help us.

Buddhism points to that which cannot be destroyed by external means. One must have peace from within, from the bottom of one's life. No one can find it for you. You must find it for yourself. Since no one can give it to you, once you have it no one can take it away. The light shines from within. When Tokusan was given the candle, he depended upon it to guide him on his way. However, Ryutan blew out the candle.

In your life you should not depend upon external "candles." Yes, they do give off light but they are not dependable. A wind might blow them out. What is to be done? Buddhism teaches freedom, and freedom only comes when you are not attached to external things. You must become yourself and then you discover the true life which has an internal light that can never be blown out.

WHO ARE YOU?

An individual person is the sum total of many aspects—material, mental, and spiritual. All these parts constitute a totality. However, take all this apart and what is left? There is no person as such. Buddhism enables one to transcend, by one's own will and one's parts. Even the "will" is transcended. In this state of enlightenment there is the full realization of the totality of life and we become one with the universe.

When we do not understand who we are, our egos create many problems. We want this and we want that. We expect other people to meet our expectations. If they don't, we are upset. How can we free ourselves from greed and anger? Buddha taught how in three steps. First, listen. Listen to the experience of others. Listen not only with the ears but with the eyes, with the body, and with the mind. Second, understand and think carefully. What is the real cause of trouble in daily life? Third, we can transcend through acceptance, regardless of what we are—black, white, short, fat, tall, or skinny—nothing is wrong. It is absolute. Each has its own unique value.

Look within and see who you are. After taking away all the parts, who are you? You are absolute totality, one with the universe. When we become one, there is no trouble. So look within yourself. What is the meaning and purpose of your life. Who are you?

BASHO'S STAFF

Zenji Basho, a famous Chinese Buddhist teacher, said to his disciples, "If you have a staff, I will give you one; if you don't have a staff, I will take it away from you."

The point of this story is concerned with the "staff." What is the staff that Zenji Basho is talking about? Long ago, traveling monks always carried a long stick or staff. It was used for protection and as a guide. In some places there were no roads; the staff was a protection against snakes and wild animals that were plentiful in the woods. Also, when a monk came to a stream he frequently didn't know how deep it was; and he could cross using the staff to measure the depth. So a staff, then, represents a guidepost. Everyone has a staff, even modern man.

Do you have a staff? A guideline by which you live? If you have one, you often become attached to this staff. If you think, "I have a staff," then you become dependent on that staff. This is what Basho is talking about. Zenji Basho is telling you not to become attached. He is saying, "I will give you the real staff." This real staff is formless and colorless. It is a guideless guide, a staffless staff. This means that in the reality of your life there is no rigid, unchanging truth. The truth is not static. Truth is always dynamic.

Truth changes because everything changes. For example, steak tastes good. Yes, generally speaking, steak is good, but if you get an ulcer steak is not good. Yesterday's truth may not be true today. In order to overcome rigidity, Zenji Basho points out that the way of Buddhism is to be free from "good and bad," "having and not having," "is and is-not." You must transcend duality because reality, life, truth are always changing. This is the path to freedom and a continuously fresh, dynamic life. Zenji Basho points to this path with his staffless staff.

EMPTINESS

Emptiness is a central teaching in Buddhism. The sutras constantly refer to it in various ways (e.g. "mu," "ku," "sunyata"). The term "emptiness" is not meant to negate things, instead it points out the essence of all things. It refers to an absolute state of no things as such. This means that no thing is fixed or static. In other words, everything changes.

Emptiness is a process, a function. Life is also a process; life is always moving on. To be alive is to be in a state of constant change. To flow with this change is to live a life that is creative and full of joy. If we do not flow with this change, life becomes monotonous. When asked, "How are you doing?" we reply, "Nothing new; just the same daily routine." Work and home life seem dead: no stimulation or inspiration.

Since life is a process, we are always doing something. It is nice when one can find something he wants to do, rather than has to do. However, even with something you have to do, if you accept it and do it, there is satisfaction. I remember a window washer who said that people laughed at him and asked him how he could stand such a boring job. His answer was, "I feel a lot of satisfaction when each window is cleaned." This is a Buddhist attitude. Collecting the garbage or washing windows is no different from any other occupation. If one does the work willingly, there is joy. Emptiness is process; this means that something is always being finished and something else is always beginning. One feels satisfaction with the completed accomplishment and is excited by the start of something new.

Emptiness is what makes life interesting. If there were no process or change occurring—how dull! No change implies the opposite of life, everything being stagnant and dead. I enjoyed playing cards the other night. With each deal different cards came; every deal was new. Of course, there are set rules to play by, but the cards are different each time. Sometimes the cards are good and sometimes they are not so good. The change is what makes playing cards so much fun.

Changes make life so interesting. This can be applied to our health. To be healthy is good; there is not much good in sickness. However, sickness is good in one sense. If you are always healthy, you do not appreciate being healthy. When you get sick, then you really appreciate good health. How about when the wife gets sick? Then the husband really realizes what it takes to keep things running smoothly in the house. Usually we take routine things for granted and we lack appreciation. So it is with everything else. Consider recession in the economic world. Some people suffer because of recession but from a broader perspective, recession is good in that it makes people realize that the economy is not always perfect; there are ups and downs.

Life is full of both suffering and joy. Change makes a person aware of this reality. This change can help a person realize the real values in life. This change is called emptiness. It is also called the doctrine of Impermanence; that is, nothing is permanent. This is the essence of the whole universe; it is the essence of our lives. Life moves and changes and that is why it is called empty. Emptiness means freshness; it means each moment of life is ever new, ever changing.

LOOK WITHIN

In the world news we hear about victims of war, starvation, terrorism, and other unspeakable things. Some people might ask, "Why do such terrible things happen?" There are many causes. Perhaps there are a thousand causes. We don't have to look just at the world news. We have plenty of suffering and cruelty in our own home towns. And we don't have to look only at our home towns—how about in our own lives and our own homes? There are no homes without problems. Let's look into our own hearts and minds. Any hate? Greed? Stupidity?

It is easy to see somebody else's faults. Our eyes are opened toward the outside but they are closed toward the inside. We see external things but we do not look within. We feel we are victimized and controlled by our environment. Why do we get upset? Why do we complain idly? It is because of external factors. "He did that, and that's why I became like this." We are always blaming other people, always blaming conditions, and always blaming something else. We never look deep inside ourselves because we do not live our own lives. Many people have not found their centers, their true selves. When we look within we become aware of our own brutality, our own ignorance, unkindness, and immorality. When we see these qualities in the world we criticize and condemn. But what about ourselves?

Buddha's teaching was to look into one's own life instead of looking outward at the world of others. When one looks within, one becomes more humble and more kind. Supposing one thinks deeply and looks into one's life and concludes, "Well, I have no unkindness, no ugly thoughts, no brutality. I am good and I want to do something good for others." Well, what good can one really do for others? Some people are so altruistic. Others are so selfish. Either extreme—altruism or selfishness—is wrong. In both, one has forgotten to live his own true life. Neither an inferiority complex nor a superiority complex helps us to live freely.

We should live like the sun. The sun has no intentions such as, "Unless I come out and shine upon the world, people will be cold and sad—so I should shine for the sake of the people." The sun just is. The sun shines and everybody is happy. How nice! It is the same with flowers. A rose never imitates any other flower; a rose is always a rose, a lily is always a lily.

Be yourself. Listen to the inner voice. Buddhism teaches us to live an authentic life which is truth itself. You must live your life. This does not mean that you must detach yourself from others. Although you live in a relative world and have to do things with other people, you still can be the master of the situation anytime, anywhere.

Some people go to their temple with a "Well, I'm just a guest, I'm just visiting" attitude. That's all right, but since you are there the temple is yours. Be useful. Be the center of the whole temple, the center of the whole congregation. If someone needs help, why not take the initiative and help. When you are the center, there is tremendous joy and creativeness.

Don't be just a visitor in life. Be aware of what is needed. Don't be an outsider. Even the first time you go somewhere, be useful since you are there—instead of standing alone or sitting uncomfortably. Do things sincerely and with life. You are a living thing, not just a dead log or dead flesh. Your spirit must be dynamically alive. You do, not because you have to or you ought to, but because you can't help but do. Life can be enthusiastic, very beautiful, one with all other people.

When people get together and do things together, all become one. Just as American Indians sit down and all smoke from the same peace pipe and become real brothers; so we become one when we eat together and do things together. In the Japanese tea ceremony, everybody drinks tea from the same bowl. I think that communion in Christianity, to eat Christ's flesh, to drink Christ's blood, means to become one with Him.

This oneness is true not only among people but also between people and all things. Take a flower, for example. The flower is living. If the leaves are drooping, water is needed. It's thirsty. When you see this you have a communication with the flower; the flower and you are one.

This is true of everything else in the world. By looking within, you become aware of and one with all things. Buddhism teaches you how to live from the inside to the outside. Look within and live your true life.

NIRVANA DAY

February 15 is Nirvana Day. On this day Gautama Buddha, lying between two sala trees and surrounded by many followers and friends, passed on. His final words to those gathered around him were, "After I am gone, the teachings will be your guide. Be true to yourself. Those who practice my teachings and live the teachings are always by me, close to me. But even though one is beside me, if he does not practice the teaching, he is not near me. All things and all lives are constantly changing, passing from one state to another. All are subject to this universal law of change. I am no exception; my final day is here. Since all things change it does not make any difference if my physical body passes away. This body is not the Buddha; enlightenment is the Buddha. Do not concern yourselves with my passing away but concern yourselves with your own enlightenment. We are all one in enlightenment. Make yourselves your own light." Those were the last words he spoke. On February 15 all Buddhists throughout the world have a memorial service. We rededicate ourselves to follow his footsteps and attain enlightenment.

The phrase "to transcend birth and death" often appears in Buddhist scriptures. This means that life and death are different phases of the same process. A continuous birth of life takes place and at the same time a continuous dying. Living and dying are the same thing. It is the same life, just different phases of the same existence. Just as a flower blooms and scatters seeds in the same process of life. Budding is not the beginning and flowering the end. The end is the beginning. The beginning is the end. However, we are so attached to the sadness of separation that we feel birth is fine and death is bad. In the last analysis, we should not be surprised or afraid of death.

The Buddha said, "Sickness and death are unavoidable in life because we are one with nature." The continuous changing of things is natural. Why do we think that death is only a sad event? Death is not something to fear. As we are courageous in living and creating, so we should be about death. Transcending life and death is not to become disinterested in or detached from life. Everything has meaning and fulfillment. We should always be ready to die, able to say "thank you for everything" and quietly, naturally, and peacefully say "goodbye." Even at the last moment of life this undisturbed mind is a beautiful thing. I think this was the Buddha's last teaching. We should learn and have this understanding and attitude in all things in our everyday lives.

FIVE EVILS

Gautama Buddha analyzed his own life and delved into the causes of his own problems and sufferings. He saw that his troubles resulted from five sources. These five sources or evils were later expounded upon in the Eternal Life sutra. They are described as competition, deception, dependency, egotism, and laziness.

The first source of trouble is competition. Life is usually viewed as based on the idea of competition, where only the strong survive. People later used Darwin's work to justify that we must fight and struggle among ourselves because only the fittest will win and the weak will be destroyed. This kind of idea spread, became well developed, and formed much of today's cultural values. We can see tremendous competition in the business and political spheres all over the world. In the name of survival and progress we fight each other. Everyone wants to be a victor and not a victim. Due to the great impact and influence of this idea, there have been advances and inventions in many fields. Yet, this competitive consciousness is an underlying cause of much suffering. Gautama Buddha saw this competition in his own life and realized that such a life would not be one of peace. The way of real peace, happiness, and freedom is not the way of competition.

The second source of trouble is deception. We have a tendency to deceive others and to be deceived by others. This is evident in the social, political, and business worlds. On a deeper personal level, we even deceive ourselves. We are not honest to ourselves and we do not live a sincere, true way of life. We compromise, rationalize, and act insincerely to avoid self criticism and guilt.

The third source of trouble is dependency. It is because of our own dependency that we have many troubles. "I depended on it to happen this way but it didn't happen as expected" or "I depended on him but he failed me." Dependency is the source of complaints and pessimism. Gautama Buddha realized this and taught the way of independent living. Independent not in the sense of being independent from other people or other things, but independent in life itself. A wife might say that she has to depend on her husband, or a person might say he has to depend on his company or on the government. Buddha is not talking in such relative terms. He is talking about being independent in living life itself—in a very subjective, existential sense.

The fourth source of trouble Gautama Buddha pointed out was egotism, the "only my way is right" type of attitude. There is no need to emphasize the presence of this selfish egotism in all of us. We disregard others and do things at the expense of others, but such a way of life does not lead to real peace and happiness.

The fifth source of trouble is laziness. We have to realize that we must exert effort in order to accomplish anything. Gautama knew we had to overcome laziness in our lives. We must work to create our lives—to realize our potentialities to the fullest.

The Eternal Life sutra describes these five sources of trouble that are contrary to a peaceful, meaningful life. Gautama was such a deep introspector that he saw these five wrongs in his own life. It is important to emphasize that Gautama Buddha was a person. Some people think that Buddha was some kind of deity or superhuman being. As a human being, Buddha suffered and had troubles. He still experienced "negative" feelings. For example, he still experienced the feeling of anger. However, the anger ceased right away; he got upset but the negative feeling did not control him very long. This time factor is important. Some people get upset and their attitude is, "I will never forget your insult. As long as I live I will remember your insult." Such a person is trying to keep all the insults and anger for his whole life. Others might keep them for a few years, others for maybe just a couple of weeks, others for maybe just one day. The Buddha forgot it immediately.

As humans we cannot rid ourselves of all negative feelings but we can learn to transcend them. To do this the first step is to sincerely make an introspection of our own lives. We must do as the Buddha did; experience the reality of the sources of suffering in ourselves.

MAPLE LEAF

Ryokan was an outstanding calligrapher and Zen monk. During his lifetime he composed many poems. One of them concerns a maple leaf on an autumn afternoon:

Maple leaf
showing front
showing back
falling down

In the Japanese language, this is very poetic. It suffers somewhat when translated into English but the meaning can still be understood. When Ryokan saw the maple leaf falling he could not help but talk to that leaf and say, "How wonderful you are. You don't just show the front and try to hide the back. How natural you are. I thought I was a monk with no double life but I realize that there still exists in me a desire to show the front and hide the back. But maple leaf, to you the front and the back are just the same—no pretensions, no ego, no artificiality. How nice. If I live like you, front and back do not make any difference. I am I."

Ryokan was inspired by the maple leaf and bowed in respect to it.

BASIC CONSCIOUSNESS

The main purpose of Buddhism is to find oneself. This means to be able to go into the basic consciousness of life. Ordinarily we move and live our daily lives only within the context of human consciousness: likes and dislikes, good and bad, and right and wrong. We see everything dichotomized; everything is compared in the process of competition. In such a dualistic world we have no serenity. In order to attain serenity and real peace in life we must go beyond the comparative world into our basic consciousness. This basic consciousness is called Buddha nature, or the world of the Buddha.

What is this world of the Buddha? Consider an analogy of waves on a lake. The waves appear and disappear according to conditions and causes of each moment. However, deep in the water, serenity prevails. Deeper the water, the more serene it is. The surface of your daily life is like the waves. It continually appears and disappears according to where you are and what you are doing. However, deep within your life there is a world of basic consciousness that external commotion cannot disturb and where you can maintain peace and serenity in all things. Although you do live in a relative world with a spouse, friends, and fellow workers, the important thing is for subject and object to be harmonized—to become "one." Each word, action, and thought comes from the basic consciousness where all life is one.

Your life can be smooth, peaceful and calm in spite of the many things you deal with. In the relative world there are anger, greediness, and many idle complaints. Being human, you have negative emotions; but if you are aware you can always return to basic consciousness. Through study and discipline you can overcome your petty self and realize this basic consciousness which is the Buddha nature within all of us.

SIMPLICITY

Buddhism means to learn simplicity. Life is simple and therefore beautiful. It is just as birds sing and flowers bloom—very natural, very simple. Life should not be analyzed. The intellect analyzes. But analysis and intellectualization will not bring peace to life, will not bring enlightenment.

Enlightenment is the direct, intuitive knowing of who one is. This is Buddhism. All the teachings can be reduced to: know yourself. To know oneself is to know that this very self is constantly changing. Life is a continuous becoming. It is not something you possess. Realizing this, you live a new life each day. Live life directly and simply. A flower is beautiful because it blooms without pretension, without artificiality. Blooming is reality; blooming is life. Blooming is the means and the end. This is how it should be in your life, too. This reminds me of a question someone asked Picasso, "Why do you paint in such a way? It is so hard to understand!" Picasso replied, "Don't ask me. Ask the bird why it sings."

Why do birds sing? Why do flowers bloom? Why does rain fall? It is life's expression. Life is like a spring gushing forth from within the earth. From the bottom of life, continuous new life springs out—so simple, so clean. Live this pure life. Drink at this spring of life and live accordingly, without pretension, without artificiality. It is this kind of simplicity that Buddhism teaches.

THE NATURAL WAY

Buddhism can be described as "The Great Natural Way." Many people think that the natural way means, "I like this; I like that." In other words, to be natural means to act according to our ordinary selfish ways. Other people think that the Way is something special. They think that it is to be found outside of everyday thoughts. They think that a special Way, per se, exists. If they are sincere seekers, they want to find and follow this Way. However, Buddhism teaches that the Way is neither a carefree, selfish way nor is it some other-worldly "special" way. It is simply the *natural* Way. Let me clarify what is meant by this natural way.

Consider the analogy of attending a wedding ceremony. When people go to a wedding, they all wear special clothes—a nice suit or fancy dress and of course, polished shoes. In the 1960s, the hippies' way was to protest against traditional formality. They said, "Why do we have to wear ties? Why shine our shoes? Why trim our hair so often?" This protest against society's formalities spread so widely that it became a habitual, customary way of dressing. There is nothing wrong with informality.

However, both formality and informality are man-made ways; they are both man-made criteria by which we judge people and set standards. In our society there is usually a front way and a back way. The front way is the formal or public way; the back way is the informal or private way. In our social lives we often do things because we feel we should, or must. "I should do it this way. If I do it in another way, people will laugh at me or criticize me." This is artificial. In contrast, Buddhism is a very natural, free way; there is no front and no back. There is no good or bad. The natural Way is not a man-made way. It is the Way that comes from our life itself. Just as a spring gushes up from the earth, there are no set rules. The spring has no particular way it must gush up; water just comes out naturally.

When the earth warms up, the flower blooms. This is natural. We want to control nature too much. For example, we want to have Easter lilies bloom at Easter so we put the lilies in a hot house to force them to bloom earlier. In warm climates, the lilies must be put under refrigeration to slow them down in order to have them bloom on Easter.

Our lives should not have such artificiality. We should be ourselves, just as we are in our everyday lives. However, this everyday or natural self tends to imply a carefree, undisciplined way. To be natural does not mean to be able to do whatever one wants. Most of us think of "self" only in terms of the ego self. In Buddhism, the natural self is not the ego self. The natural self is the self that is never defiled or controlled by the environment. It is the self expressed in a poem by Rev. Akegarasu:

My thought is thought,
It is never myself.
I had thought that my thought is myself,
but now I'm aware
I made a terrible mistake.

My experience is experience. It
is never myself. I had thought
that experience is
myself, but now I'm aware
I made a terrible mistake.

My feelings are feelings,
they are never myself.
I had thought that my feelings
are myself,
but now I'm aware
I made a terrible mistake.

My will is will. It is
never myself.
I had thought
that my will is myself, but now
I'm aware I made
a terrible mistake.

My wishes are wishes,
they are never myself.
I had thought that my wishes

are myself,
but now I'm aware
I made a terrible
mistake.

My deeds are deeds,
they are never myself.
I had thought that my deeds are myself,
but now I'm aware
I made a terrible mistake.

But then
who am I?

Yes, it is true, that through
thought, experience, feeling,
will, wish, and deed
I manifest myself,
but also I manifest myself
when I break out
of all of these.

I am not such a limited self,
conceptualized self,
as to exist apart from others!
I alone
am the most noble:
I embrace the cosmos.

What an indescribable, subtle
existence I am!—I cannot in
speaking or writing
put down who I am!

I always touch this indescribable self,
always follow this indescribable self.
Truth is here.

There is something beyond our feelings, experiences, or wishes. This is the life or self that lives the natural Way. Expressed in a concrete person, it is the Buddha. The natural Way is the Buddha's Way, your Way. Since we are all unique individuals, expression of this Way is different for each of us; yet, the essence is the same.

Explaining the Way is difficult. Words cannot touch it directly but can only point to it. Do not become attached to words or to what has been said. Explanations are only motivators, pointing you in a direction. You yourself have to find the Way.

GATELESS GATE

A student asked his teacher, "How do I enter the Buddha's world? Where is the gate?" The teacher answered, "You enter through the gateless gate."

In this dialogue, the idea of a gate is important. A gate, as we know it, is something through which one enters. It divides the inside from the outside. But in the world of Buddhism, what is a gate? Unless you understand what kind of gate is meant, you cannot understand the dialogue.

Inside and outside are only conceptual. Wherever you are can be inside or outside. Before understanding the Dharma teachings, you feel you are outside. Once you are inside, you realize there never was a gate. There is no gate as such. Yet in another sense there still is a gate. This is why it is called the gateless gate. The Dharma or truth is everywhere. The gate is everywhere. There is no gate to go through; you are in already. It is often said that one "attains" enlightenment. What is this kind of enlightenment that one can attain? It is a self-made enlightenment. There is no such thing. Enlightenment is everywhere. You are in it but you don't know it. One does not attain enlightenment; instead, one finds oneself in enlightenment. You, I, the whole world are in enlightenment, but because of our ignorance we are unable to see this world of enlightenment. If we open our eyes, we see we are in it. Then there is no gate to go through. There's no outside and no inside. This is the gateless gate.

BUDDHA'S GIFT

Kasyapa was one of the Buddha's great disciples. He was one of the leaders of the Sangha after Buddha passed away. Ananda, another famous disciple, asked Kasyapa, "Besides the robe and bowl (these were symbols of the Dharma transmission) what else did the Teacher pass on to you?" Kasyapa said, "Ananda!" Ananda replied, "Yes?"

Although Ananda was a devoted and faithful disciple, he represents the unenlightened person. Kasyapa represents the enlightened individual. Besides the robe and bowl, Ananda wanted to know what else Kasyapa had received, perhaps some secret doctrine or teaching. To Kasyapa such a question was foolish. What the Buddha left was the way of direct communication. When Kasyapa called "Ananda!", Ananda answered,"Yes?" There was no lapse, no time for thinking. In the way of true communication there is no thinking, no scheming. There is oneness. It is direct and very immediate. It was this direct, true communication that the Buddha taught Kasyapa. True teaching is awareness of this oneness, this immediate communication between all beings. Every word and every action between people, if done with awareness, makes explanations unnecessary.

If there is a direct, intimate communication between yourself and in whatever you are engaged, then there is oneness. For example, food is life, the life of the eater is food. There should be a feeling of untold gratitude towards food; it is because of food that you are able to exist. Food and the eater are one in life, the essence is the same. This realization of oneness is Buddhism. It involves the highest type of communication and respect. If your life is realized in this sense—between you and work, friends, and clothing—you would see that the whole world supports you. You exist because of others; everything supports your life. This totality, this oneness evokes a gratitude and a great joy beyond explanation. If two persons become one in love or in trust, words are not necessary. Their entire life is communicated by a pat on the shoulder, a wink, the touching of toes beneath the table. Even between two persons on an entirely human level there can be a feeling of oneness. How much more so if you communicate directly with all things you encounter in the world. This intimate oneness is a tremendous thing. This is what the Buddha left to Kasyapa, to all of us.

MIDDLE WAY

There are many teachings in Buddhism. However, it could be said that the basic teaching of Buddhism is the Middle Way.

To explain the Buddhist meaning of Middle Way is difficult because the word "middle" suggests "between" and people misinterpret the Middle Way as a point or path between two extremes; in other words, as compromise. Compromise as appeasement has bad connotations. Everyone knows that nothing ever comes of appeasement in the political world.

As for problems in home life such as quarrels between husband and wife, we all feel that neither the husband's way nor the wife's way is the only way but that family life is compromise, a give and take. Similarly, in our democratic way of life, the middle way is usually understood as avoiding the extremes of one way or the other. People try to compromise between the "either/or" of Western culture.

In the world of relativity, people feel that the middle point is the way of compromise. However, the Buddhist middle point is a different realm, an entirely different dimension of life which Buddha taught. In this dimension there is a different conception of time than the usual notion of historical time. Historical time is usually considered to be a series of events, just as a straight line is a series of innumerable points. A series of events, say from the time of the Greeks to today, is called history.

However, the Buddhist concept of time is not historical time. It is not serial points of moments. The past is already gone. The future is yet to come. The reality of time is just this present, this very moment. Buddhism goes even further and warns us not to cling to or be captivated by the midpoint of the vast past and vast future. This is because the middle point is a flowing, continuous moving process. As soon as we say, "This is the middle point," it has gone already and another new middle point is already existing.

The Middle Way is life itself. We live today, and we live this very moment. In this very moment is the entirety of history. When we explain that America declared its independence in 1776 or Columbus discovered the American continent in 1492, we see those series of years through time. However to me, all those hundreds of years of history are not in serial points but in this very instant. In me there are wonderful great civilizations, wonderful Indian histories; the American independence, and the French revolution. All are present in this one moment in me. Only in explanation, only in the conceptualized world does serial time exist. Reality is this very moment. Buddha exists in this very moment, not 2,500 years ago but now in me.

This way of looking at life is important because we are living now. We cannot live in the past; we cannot live in the future. If you try to, you will have nothing but complaints. The important thing is how you are living now. That is the very reason Gautama Buddha did not speculate into the unknowable past or unknowable future. He emphasized the present, the importance of each day and the importance of each moment, the now. This is the Middle Way.

WATER

In sutras, Buddha often uses the example of water. Water can be used to teach us many things. Water can illustrate that in spite of individual differences, we all share a oneness of life. The uniqueness of our individual selves can be compared to the many different kinds of waves that can be formed in the water.

On a stormy day along the seashore, giant waves crash against the cliff. The waves can even break off granite from the walls of the cliff. The same water can also be very quiet. On a peaceful morning, the waves are small and the water is calm. Regardless of size and activity of the waves, their essence is the same. Although shapes of the individual waves are unique, all waves are made of water. Time and place do not matter. It does not matter if we are referring to water existing today, in ancient times, or in the future. It does not matter if the water is in Europe, Asia, or the United States, water is the same everywhere. It is universal. Our individual selves are like the many different kinds of waves. We are different—some of us are black, some are white, some are brown, and some are yellow. We are different in color and different in shape. Each individual is uniquely different from each other. Yet the essence of life is one. When one realizes this oneness of life, he becomes peaceful. He does not fight against conditions but is free to become "one" with such conditions.

In the same way, water changes its form according to the shape of the receptacle it is in. When water is put into a round bowl, it becomes round. Water is not stubborn, as some people are; water adapts itself according to the conditions. Yet, at the same time it remains water and never changes its essential nature. We too can be flexible and yet not lose our essential nature. To be yielding is not necessarily a sign of weakness. Water is soft and meek and yet it has a dynamic power to turn great dynamos. At the same time, water is humble. It always seeks the lowest level. It never tries to be on top or show off but instead goes to the bottom. The lowest level is a safe, natural, and peaceful place.

The mind of the Buddha is often said to be a great ocean-mind. Buddha's mind is large enough to receive and accept all things just as the ocean receives all the dirty waters of the rivers and purifies them. If we have a great ocean-mind, we can take in all things and not be upset by them. There are no tensions or complexes of any kind in the great ocean-mind.

Water is Buddhistic; we can see many teachings in the nature of water.

PURPOSELESS PURPOSE

Our way of life in American culture is purposeful and goal-oriented. If there is no purpose in something we judge it useless. In today's modern life a purposeless action is considered meaningless.

A reporter from a local newspaper came to our house to interview my wife about the Japanese tea ceremony. This reporter continuously asked, "What is the meaning? What for? Why do you do that? What is the purpose of that?" This kind of question was directed at everything in the making of tea—at every gesture, every implement. Without thinking or deliberating, my wife finally replied, "No meaning. Meaningless meaning. It is purposeless. Purposeless purpose." The interviewer was very much intrigued by this reply. On the other hand, my wife was intrigued by the reporter's obsession with meaning and purpose. Why did the reporter need to continuously ask, "What is the meaning, the purpose?" Later, my wife confided to me that, although she had never thought of it before, she and the newspaper reporter were living in very different worlds.

In addition to purposefulness, there is another side to life: purposelessness. Both aspects are true. Being purposeful is well suited to our materialistic society; in order to accomplish things, we must have purpose. Yet the purposeless way is also a beautiful way: a flower blooms, a bird sings, a child plays. A biologist might claim that a flower blooms to attract insects which then spread the pollen. But the flower itself cannot help but bloom as it does—there is no intention. Life itself is purposeless. Water flows effortlessly. It cannot help but flow—that is the way it is. Effortless effort, purposeless purpose, this is the real way of life. Although nothing can be accomplished without effort the Buddhist way is effortless effort.

When you love, you love. There is no purpose. Why do we ask for meaning? Of course, in our social life we do ascribe "meanings" to things and events; but with regard to the essence of life, it just is. If we do something from the beginning with purpose and meaning, then it becomes quite rigid. Meanings and reasons may be given later but the doing is the purpose itself. If we continually live in the midst of purposeful, directed activity, soon we feel pressured and "must" enters our lives. There is no naturalness. This is the very reason Buddha taught that the essence of life just is, as it is.

We should learn the purposeless way of life—purposeless doing. A utilitarian person would say, "That is nonsense!" However, nonsense is important in life. Too much intelligence or too much efficiency can create trouble. So, we must learn non-intelligence, which is super-intelligence.

True life is purposeless. To realize this truth of life is Buddhism. In one sense that is purpose, in another sense it is purposeless. Life is always like that; it is inclusive. If we analyze it, it becomes two, but the reality is always one. Here and now—time and space—this very point is all-inclusive. Only when we analyze do we have different directions. True reality is natural and purposeless.

Why not enjoy the naturalness of life? The doing itself is the end fulfillment. In this state everything is at ease. This is the state of meaningless meaning. It has no meaning and yet in another sense it has tremendous meaning. It is life itself. When one just is, one forgets all other things, one forgets the self. It is said, "To learn Buddhism is to know oneself. To know oneself is to forget oneself." One just is. This state is perfect naturalness. A state of meaningless meaning and purposeless purpose. This is what the Buddha taught.

NO MIND

In Buddhism "no mind" means that in living life you should not have a mind that controls you. There should be no mind to dictate to you. There should be no mind that says to do things in the sense of duty. "No mind" means to be yourself, just as you are—natural, with no self-conscious purposes—with no explanations. No mind means, "just is." No mind is naturalness; it is laughing; it is skiing down a slope; it is whenever you do things with your total being. When children play they put their total life into their playing. Water flows in the same way. Water has no intention of flowing. It doesn't say, "I have to flow this way; I have to flow that way."

The other day I attended a funeral service for a man who committed suicide by hanging himself in his basement. He had nothing left to live for. Why did this man hang himself? There didn't seem to be any family trouble—he had a good wife and two healthy children. But he simply lost his life. While he was living there was no life. Before he hanged himself he had already lost his life. The hanging itself was only the end result. Too bad he did not realize what true life really is.

We have too many self-conscious purposes when doing things. Our intentions lead to expectations and when these are not fulfilled and do not work out, then disappointment and regret result. These are unpleasant things in our lives. We feel hurt and this results in our hurting others. But all of life, the whole world, just is. The way of life is not "why?" Life overflows; it moves. This is the way we should do things in everyday life. Then we will often find that the doing itself is the satisfaction. When there is too much "mind" in our activities we become artificial and our lives do not flow smoothly.

Life must flow out from within and not for external reasons. It does not matter whether one's activities are approved by others or not. It does not matter if the benefit goes to someone else. If you are doing something, do it. There should be no rigid expectancies and no self-conscious intentions. This is the life of "no mind."

HOW THE BUDDHA TAUGHT

Although it is important to know *what* the Buddha taught, in another way it is more important to know *how* he taught. I talked about this recently to our temple's high school students. I started out by saying, "Today I am not going to tell you about the Buddha's teachings. These things you can read about later. Instead, let's look at how Buddha taught. He never gave answers on a silver platter. He never said, 'This is the truth; you should believe it and follow it.' On the contrary, Buddha said, 'Don't believe something just because I said it. Do not follow teachings until you test them through your own experience.' The Buddha always said to look into our own lives."

Then I asked the students, "What is the most important thing in your life?" One girl said, "My parents." We talked about the importance of parents. Another student mentioned money. I asked, "Is money the most important thing?" Everybody said, "No." However, I countered that we can't deny that money is very important. If we did not have money, we could not function in today's society. Another boy said, "Life itself is most important." "What do you mean life itself?" I asked. He must have taken biology because he answered, "Life is composed of cells." I commented, "It is important to keep your body alive and healthy." "Yes," he replied, "without a healthy body, we cannot help others." This led into exploring the value of altruism. We continued to consider many other different answers to the question of what is the most important thing in life. Although many aspects were discussed, we did not arrive at one final answer. I explained that we each have to think things out for ourselves. This is the Buddhist approach.

The Buddha never handed out teachings like a pill saying, "Here, swallow this." Instead he always asked, "Is that right? What do you think?" He offered teachings so that you could try them in your own life. He did not tabulate his teachings. His teachings were not static or statistical in form. His teachings were dynamic and always dealt with value in one's life. For instance, what is real happiness in your life? Many children are happy when their fathers give them a weekly allowance. However, when that allowance is gone by the middle of the week, they are sad. Happiness that is created by friendship lasts only as long as your friend is present. When your friend is gone, you are sad.

Does real happiness come from external things? What is the real happiness in your life? These are the kinds of challenges that the Buddha always asked. He never commanded people. In Buddhism, there is no dogma; there is no set of formal teachings. The teachings are always put within the context of an individual's experience. Understanding should come from living, not from the head. This is the Buddhist way. This is how the Buddha taught.

BODHI DAY

December 8 is Bodhi Day. On this day, after years of effort, Siddartha Gautama meditated under the pipal tree and attained enlightenment. He was then called "Buddha," which means the "awakened one." This was the beginning of Buddhism.

Siddartha was born as a crown prince. He had wealth, power—everything an ordinary man would want. However, there was a great deal of internal struggle in the prince. He wanted to know, really know, about life and how its sufferings could be overcome. All men are subject to suffering caused by illness, old age, death, and sufferings arising from separation from loved ones and forced contact with disliked people. There are many sufferings which arise from desires that cannot be satisfied.

Siddartha meditated on the nature of suffering and concluded that the root of suffering is ignorance. This ignorance can appear in many ways—as egotistic selfishness, as stupidity, or as greed. There were many temptations for young Siddartha. A story is told that while in meditation, three beautiful sisters came and danced for him and beseeched him to return to his father's palace and enjoy life. Demons appeared and threatened his life—avoiding fear was also a temptation. Many temptations came and he subdued them, one after another. But as he subdued one temptation, another appeared. He subdued that temptation, and another appeared. They were endlessly coming, temptation after temptation, there was no end to them.

Siddartha wondered why. He realized that temptations were not coming from anywhere; they were all within himself. When he realized that he was the source of all temptation, then duality was transcended. This great discovery was his enlightenment.

On the morning of December 8, as the morning star was brightly shining, Siddartha experienced that the root of suffering was within him. He was it. This was great enlightenment. As he was the root of all temptation, so he was also the one to master these temptations. He saw the truth of the reality of life. This is Buddhism.

SELFLESSNESS

The purpose in Buddhism is to overcome the self, overcome the duality of things, overcome multiplicity and become one's true self. A stronger way of stating this is, one should become totally selfless. We have trouble because we cannot become ourselves; that is, we cannot become selfless. Selflessness is something like putting water into a bottle. If you fill the bottle half full, cork and shake it, you can hear the noise of the water. However, if you fill the bottle completely, leaving no air space, then there is no sound when you shake it. No matter how you toss it there is no noise. Of course, when the bottle is completely empty there is no noise, but there is no water either. The self can be compared to these three conditions: no water in a bottle, partially filled, or completely filled. Which are you? No water in the bottle? Half filled? Or completely filled which is "emptiness"? Yes, this kind of emptiness is when the water goes completely to the top. The bottle has weight but there is no noise. Selflessness is when you are filled to the top. It is when you are fulfilled. There is no noise, no self. You must be all empty, or in other words, you must be fully, wholly fulfilled to the top. You become selfless.

All the small, petty things in you make up your "small" self. They are the sensations, perceptions and ideas that come from the outside and make noise in you. You should not be empty in the ordinary sense of the word but you should attain complete fullness; this is Buddhist emptiness or Buddhist selflessness. You are the one who occupies the whole world. So no one can crush you. There is no small, petty self to be disturbed. Even if you are shaken, there is no noise. When you are completely fulfilled, then you must even forget that fulfillment. Forget enlightenment. Forget Buddha. Then you are like a bottle filled with water—so settled down, so heavy. You become one with this whole universe. This is enlightenment; this is selflessness.

NOBILITY

When Gautama Buddha attained Enlightenment, he declared, "I alone am noble above heaven and below heaven." This means, "I alone am noble in the whole universe." This was an expression of his discovery of his true self. Every being possesses such a noble essence. In Western terminology it is the divinity in all of us. However, most of the time our ego gets the best of us and our nobility or divine quality is hidden deep down within us. Gautama discovered this nobility in himself and he lived that nobility. All beings are pure and good. Good in an absolute, not relative sense. It is good not as compared to bad. Without comparing, beyond the sense of relativity, we all have the noble quality in us. To be aware of this nobility in us is an important thing.

When I was a small boy, my grandfather used to say, "You belong to the Kubose family and our family has been a noble family of long standing. If you do a shameful thing, it is a shame to the whole Kubose family. You should remember that. A boy of a good family does not do shameful things." Many young children were told such things and our young minds were impressed. I am grateful for such teachings from my grandfather. To impress a young mind with such nobleness, whether nobleness of family or nobleness of a person, is very important. I sometimes hear parents telling their children, "You are bad" or "You are no good." This is a negative approach; it is the wrong kind of scolding for a child. It would be much better to make the child aware of the nobleness of himself or his family. If a boy misbehaves, he could be told that a son of a good family does not do such things. It makes a lot of difference psychologically if he has this thought of being a child of a noble family instead of having his smallness or evilness emphasized. In fact, the latter emphasis would actually contribute towards creating such negative qualities. We should always try to emphasize the nobleness of a person. This is particularly important at a young age, when the mind is so open and receptive. This kind of teaching sticks in the mind of a young child and can influence his whole life.

Today in our midst, there is so much crime and degenerate behavior. When I read about such things in the newspaper, I always think about the quality of nobleness and how it is lacking in our society. Most people have noble thoughts and feelings but their egos get the better of them and they do not behave accordingly. A person may know it is wrong to steal or do a bad thing, but momentarily he forgets his nobility and he does the wrong thing. It is important to educate ourselves, to become aware that we have this nobility in us. All other persons and things also have this nobility. What we lack in our culture today is the awareness of nobility in others. There does not seem to be any emphasis on such education in our society. It is lacking in our child training and in our social institutions. This is why families and our nation are in turmoil.

Awareness of the quality of nobleness in all beings is very important. It leads to a sense of oneness, to feelings of respect and humility. When Gautama Buddha declared, "I alone am noble in the whole world," this did not mean that he alone was noble. "I alone" means that each individual from his own perspective is the most noble. Buddha's declaration of his nobility is the declaration of every being; everyone should have this thought of nobleness of himself or herself. When one is aware of the nobleness in oneself, one cannot help but be noble. He cannot do wrong things. This is the foundation and basis of Buddhist teachings. This is religion in the Buddhist sense.

THE FRESH, CREATIVE LIFE

Many people talk about being busy. Some people say to me, "Oh, you are so busy that I hesitate to tell you or ask you something." In reality, a person is really not busy at all. We cannot do two things at the same time. We are always engaged in only one thing at a time. If we can realize and live this truth, then we will know why the Buddha stressed non-attachment.

You should not become attached to what has happened in the past because life is a process, a becoming; every moment is a new life, a new flow. Of course, past experiences can serve as a good reference when planning what you wish to do tomorrow, or in your lifetime. But when you do it, do one thing at a time. Put everything into it and when it is finished, it is finished. Then start a new thing. What I am talking about is how to take care of your mind. If your mind flows like water you will not experience fatigue. Getting tired is usually due more to mental fatigue than to physical fatigue. Becoming angry or emotionally upset is due to attachment to the past— to something that happened earlier. If someone criticizes you, you become upset. "I didn't do that, but he said that I did." It is the attachment to past words, deeds, or thoughts that hinders what you do in the present.

Observe children in their play, they are completely absorbed in what they are doing. Adults can be the same way. When we do something we enjoy, we forget all other things and become completely involved in whatever we are doing. Those minutes and hours are really beautiful. Even the thought of enjoyment is totally forgotten. We become "nothing." The state of nothing is not empty; it is full of life. One's whole life is involved in what one is doing and the self is forgotten. At such times we don't get tired because there is creativity, which is the realization of life itself.

We can quickly recover from physical tiredness by resting but mental fatigue is another matter. Such things as worry, jealousy, and hatred are hard to eliminate; they linger in our minds. Emptying our minds provides a rest. We can accomplish this by doing things one at a time. Do it one hundred percent so that nothing else takes place. This kind of life is important.

The Buddha said, "All things are in constant change; nothing is permanent." This means that life is a process, a continuous becoming. In a limited, relative sense, today is a continuation of yesterday but in reality, today is a totally new day. We live a new life every moment. Why spoil this new life? We should make this new life the best, most beautiful and most meaningful. But most of us spoil this new life because of yesterday's unpleasant affairs. Something disagreeable that happened last night still bothers us. I know some couples who do not talk to each other for two or three days. We are human, so we have these kinds of feelings. We are unable to wipe them out, unable to forget. Even if we remember to try, it is hard to forget something that has hurt us deeply. However, it is a discipline, if you want to call it discipline, wherein one is able to transcend anger and quarrels, and to start a new day. To be able to control one's own mind is to be able to live each day as a new day. This is what non-attachment means. This is the basis for the fresh, creative life. Do not defile your beautiful life. That is the very reason the Buddha always referred to the lotus flower. It grows and blooms in a muddy pond but the lotus is never defiled by its environment, the muddiness. It always keeps its own purity. When the sun comes, the lotus opens its leaves and buds and fully appreciates the sunshine. Let us all live this kind of fresh, creative life.

EQUALITY

The Buddhist concept of equality is expressed in a sutra which says, "Difference is equal; equal means different." Buddhism teaches that all beings are equal. However, this equality does not mean that all beings are the same. For example, a table is a piece of furniture on which to put things. The top of the table is beautiful and the legs are underneath supporting the top. The legs are usually not visible but there is no table without legs. The legs are just as important as the top. Each has its unique position to fulfill. There is no actual superiority or inferiority. All are equal. So it is with all things.

We live in a democratic society and this can be taken to imply that we are all equal, all the same. However, there is no democracy in the sense that all are literally equal. We are not equal in the sense of everyone being the same. It is only in a convenient sense that all citizens are considered equal. The President has his duties to perform and so does everyone else—congressmen, city officials, garbage collectors. Garbage collectors are just as important as city officials. If the garbage collectors strike and do not collect the garbage for months, the city would be a stinky, dirty place. Garbage collectors are important and we should respect them just as we do the mayor or governor. The work is different but the quality, the value, is the same. Difference is equality. This kind of perspective can be seen in the phrase, "byodo soku sabetsu" which says, "equal means different." This view is also present in

the Zen saying, "shiki soku ze ku" or "all things are empty."
Here, empty means everything. This kind of paradoxical
expression is used to try and express the reality of things.
Truth or reality is paradoxical. The ideas of right and wrong,
for example, are exactly opposite, but right and wrong are
equal or the same in the sense that if there is no wrong there
is no right. Just as light and darkness exist only in relationship
to each other. If there is all darkness, there can be no light.
Darkness exists only in relation to brightness. Wisdom cannot
exist without ignorance. Many examples can be mentioned.
There can be no husband without a wife; no teacher without
a student. It is because things are different but equal that there
is a oneness of all things.

Husband and wife are different people; they have different
personalities and usually have different domestic duties. The
children are also different and have their different duties and
privileges. Yet, wife, husband, and children together become
one and form a whole. All are different but at the same time
one and the same. In a family there are many members, but
they are one in the name of the family. To realize this oneness
and to live accordingly is the Buddhist way. This teaching
is expressed in the Buddhist quotation, "One is many and
many is one." This kind of perspective or way of life can be
extended to all humans, in all situations—whether people are
joined together in a business, church, or country. And funda-
mentally, there is always a basic oneness because there is
universal equality in life itself.

QUIETNESS

It is important to take time to have some quiet moments in our lives. Otherwise we get caught up in the busy-ness of always having to have something going on. If it's not the TV always being on, it's the radio as soon as we get into the car. We can't even go to the bathroom or eat by ourselves without grabbing a newspaper to read.

To become quiet does not mean a negative passivity. Quietness can be a dynamic state. There are two kinds of quietness. One is dead quietness with no life in it; the other quietness is alive with awareness. We become aware of serenity in both ourselves and in the world. This happens because we see that we are one with the world. Quietness is not a turning away from the world but a realization that you are the world. During quietness you breathe together with the whole world. This is the very reason quietness is so refreshing. We have to learn to be quiet just as we have to learn to acquire certain tastes. But this quietness, once acquired, has tremendous sweetness.

FOREIGN GATES

There is an old saying: "Anything that comes from the gates is foreign." "Coming from the gates" refers to things that enter through the eyes, ears and other senses; whatever comes from outside one's self is foreign. You should not obey foreign commands. Every action, every word should come from deep within—not from external sensory stimulation.

This is an important thing in Buddhism. Instead of moving according to external influences, we must always listen to the deep inner voice and follow that voice. It is true that our daily lives are influenced and oftentimes controlled by external things. For example, we often say "I have to do such-and-such", or "I did that because he told me to!" Instead, our actions should reflect an attitude of, "I want to do such-and-such." More than that, there should be the feeling of "I can't help but do it; my life force commands me to do it."

We often react to our environment with anger. Anger is usually a reaction to the words and deeds of others. When we are upset we lose our center of life; we feel pressure. This is one of the general characteristics of modern life. We are easily upset and experience so much commotion because of our environment. Buddha always taught. Never mind your environment, never mind what others say. Just settle down deeply, firmly in your own inner life. All your actions and all your feelings must come from within.

Don't rebel against what comes to you. When you feel nervous, pressured, and start to complain about things, this is because you are moved by external things. Look into yourself. The way of Buddhism is an absolute, subjective way of life. When you live according to your inner voice, you will not become a victim of the environment. You live your own life. That is the very reason it was said, "All things that come from the gates are foreign." You should not follow foreigners; you have to be the master of your own self.

I AND THOU

In the I and Thou relationship, the so-called "I" is mostly ego. We see, hear, feel, and this "I" makes evaluations and judgments. Yet, there is another "I" behind it. Martin Buber calls it Thou. Hindus say atman. In modern terminology it might be called true self. So I and Thou could be said to correspond to ego self and true self, respectively.

There are often conflicts or contradictions between I and Thou. However, when they become completely one, then Thou is always expressed in I. The Thou may be called Universal Life whereas the "I" may be called individual life. This Thou could be deep within oneself or it could be objectified. One religion may call it God. Some call it the Absolute. Some call it Buddha. Regardless, our life is always confronted by a dialogue between I and Thou.

We must let life live. Whenever we live for our own benefit trying to make life purposive, then life becomes a difficult thing. Yes, there is a purpose and yet when we are actually doing something there is no purpose, a purposeless purpose. What a contradictory statement! Yet, that is how life actually is. Rationality and irrationality go together at the same time. Life is a contradiction, and yet this contradiction is not a contradiction. It is complementary. We are living in a relative world where "I" is the center and all things surround me in relationships. We cannot escape this relative world. Yes, it is a relative world, but totality is not relative; it is absolute. Buddhism teaches us to live an absolute life in a relative world. This is the true life where Thou and I become completely one.

SOUNDLESS SOUND

The other day a group of young Christians along with their Sunday school teachers visited the temple. As usual, I explained Buddhism to them. Later they asked various questions. One of the questions was, "What is that brown bowl on the altar?" (They were referring to a large bronze bell.) "That is a bell," I replied. "What is it for? What does it symbolize?" "Well, it doesn't exactly symbolize anything in particular. But if you wish to consider it as symbolic, then it symbolizes life. I'll let you hear the sound of the bell."

I struck the bell and everyone became *so quiet.* They listened until the very end of the sound. Then I remarked, "This is the way we begin our Buddhist services. Everyone listens to the sound of the bell, getting rid of extraneous thoughts and making their minds open and receptive. Most important, we are able to listen to the soundless sound."

One of the teachers was very taken by this idea of soundless sound. I could see it in her face. She was thinking about it and she finally asked, "What is this soundless sound?" I replied, "The soundless sound is the sound you have to hear yourself. It cannot be explained." She said, "Is there such a thing as a *soundless* sound?" I answered, "To hear the soundless sound . . . that is the Buddhist teaching." She was thinking quite hard. "Are we able to hear it?" "Yes, that is Buddhism." She persisted, "But can't you explain it *somehow*?" She was so intensely interested in that one phrase: soundless sound.

However, all I could say to her was, "The soundless sound is one thing I cannot explain to you; yet you do have the ability to hear the soundless sound."

What is the soundless sound? The bell always sits silently on a cushion. Whenever anyone strikes the bell, it creates sound. Depending upon how it is hit, different sounds are produced: high, low, short, or long. There are myriad tones contained in that bell. From the bell's point of view, it responds according to how it is struck.

There is one temple in Kyoto, Japan, which is famous for having a huge bell. On New Year's Eve it is a Japanese custom for each temple to strike its bell 108 times to send out the old year and welcome in the new year. The city of Kyoto has many Buddhist temples. Consequently, many different kinds of bells are heard on New Year's Eve. However, the bell at this one temple is so huge that if one person strikes it, hardly any sound is heard. The clapper is a huge log suspended by 16 ropes. It takes 16 priests, all swaying together, to draw back the ropes so that the log can strike the bell. This creates a most tremendous sound.

Every bell has the potential to produce hundreds of sounds and vibrations. This is also the way our life is. Each one of us is like a bell. We possess a capability of producing sounds, according to how things of the world strike against us. Some of us produce sharp tones; others produce flat tones. All these sounds and vibrations result from an interaction between ourselves and our environment. All bells and all people have the potential to produce sounds. Each bell has unexpressed tones in it. Each one of us also possesses this unexpressed music. Each individual has the potential to create his own music. We are ever ready to produce sound. This is the soundless sound. Each bell, each individual has this soundless sound.

My teacher, Rev. Akegarasu, was very interested in bells. In his house he had a collection of bells from all over the world. There were bells of every size and shape and bells made of all kinds of material—copper, clay, silver, gold. Perhaps my teacher was interested in bells because of the soundless sound each has.

As for the soundless sound itself, as I told the Sunday school teacher, it is something to be experienced, not explained. Each person can hear the soundless sound. This is religion. It does not matter if the religion is named Christianity, Buddhism, Judaism, or Islam. Religion exists for anyone who is able to hear the profound sound, the soundless sound. The world of the soundless sound is such a beautiful, magnificent world. It is unique and yet universal. Find it. Listen to it. Live it.

TURTLE IN THE GARDEN

A student saw a turtle sunning itself on a rock in Daizu's garden. The student asked the teacher, "All beings cover their bones with flesh and skin. Why does this turtle cover its flesh and skin with bones?" Master Daizu took off his sandals and covered the turtle.

In this story the student was determined to make discriminations—flesh and bones, inside and outside. Discriminating can be carried as far as one likes—is mind inside of body or is body inside of mind? But this attitude always results in arguments and explanations. Life is neither. Life is an organic, living totality. Of course there are systems of thought that can be rational, or philosophical. But life is not philosophy. Life is not rationality. Life is dynamic. Buddhism says, "Don't compare." Inside or outside doesn't matter. Be your true self. A flower is a flower. A turtle is a turtle. The turtle doesn't ponder, "Bones inside or outside?"

Daizu covered the turtle with his sandals to indicate to the student that he must get in touch with his true life and not just try to understand reality by simply explaining the phenomenal world. Of course we could propose many reasons for Daizu's actions, but the important thing is to live your true life from within. You live twenty-four hours a day. How many hours do you live a real, genuine life? You are always pushed around and influenced. You become upset when things are not going well. You become greedy when things are going well. You are always influenced by the environment, never living your true life. Buddhism teaches you to live your true life.

FORGET YOURSELF

Dogen, a famous Buddhist teacher of 13th Century Japan said, "To know Buddhism is to know oneself. To know oneself is to forget oneself."

"To forget oneself" is an interesting statement. To forget oneself does not mean to become dumbfounded. On the contrary, it is when you are doing something so intensely that you forget yourself. Doer and doing become totally one. No ego self exists. There is no self-consciousness; the ego, the pretending self, disappears. One transcends oneself. This kind of state is to forget oneself.

The "forget" in Dogen's "forget oneself" has nothing to do with memory. It is not the same thing as leaving the house and forgetting your keys. It is not a lack of consciousness either. Some time ago in a cartoon, a father was depicted lying on the couch, a newspaper over his face. The mother instructed the son to call his father for dinner. The son, seeing his father under the newspaper fast asleep, came back to the mother and reported, "Oh, Daddy is in Nirvana." The father had "forgotten" himself but this is not the enlightened "forget oneself" of Buddhism. The Buddhist forgotten self is a dynamic state. If we live life in this dynamic forgotten state, life becomes creative.

The teaching of "forget the self" or "selflessness" can also be expressed by the term "suchness." Things as they are, are in a state of suchness. When the sun comes out a flower opens up and blooms. This is how we should live, with no ego—just be. This is forgetting oneself. It is putting your whole life into whatever you do. To say, "Put your whole life into it." or "Do it with life!" does not mean being tense or straining at what you do. To be totally involved in something is quite natural. You are relaxed and yet totally aware. In such a state there is no "this" or "that" thinking. If you are thinking of something else while performing the Japanese tea ceremony, you always make a mistake. The same thing happens in chanting. Even though the verses are memorized, if some thought comes into your mind then you make a mistake.

Doing something is a wonderful thing. You can put yourself into it and forget yourself. If your mind is trained, whatever you do can be done with a single-mindedness. You are able to create a one-pointedness of the mind. When you do something, you are able to do it completely. When you go to bed you are able to sleep completely. Stillness of the body is not resting; mind totally forgotten, that is rest. You can be at rest while busy doing something. Buddhism is learning how to live by forgetting oneself.

It is characteristic in Buddhism to use negative expressions such as "forget oneself," "selflessness," or "non-self." I think this is better than a positive way of expressing things. If a positive expression is used, it limits itself. If we say, "concentrate," then we try so hard to concentrate and the self is in it. You cannot think, "I have to forget," and expect to forget. You cannot achieve the forgotten state by *trying* to forget oneself. This is a dualistic way of thinking. It implies that there is a self to be forgotten and that there is a self which does the forgetting. Instead, there is only selflessness. Selflessness is when you do something with all your heart or with your whole self—then there is no artificial or superficial self in it. In selflessness your real authentic self is revealed. Just as when a person is not trying to show it, somewhere it will reveal itself. You should love yourself; you should love life. This kind of love is necessary for you to forget yourself. It is only by actively putting yourself into the present moment that you forget yourself. When you do forget yourself, you act naturally and your true self comes out. This true self is selflessness. This is the Buddhist teaching of "forget yourself."

PERFECTION

Recently I visited a flower arrangement exhibition. One of the exhibitors was the wife of a Buddhist minister here in Chicago. She has been teaching flower arrangement for many decades and has several hundred students. Every year I admire her work but I was particularly impressed this year. Her arrangements are always very simple. This year's arrangement consisted of a single flower, a chrysanthemum. However, placed in an important position next to this single flower was a worm-eaten leaf. Usually half-dead or half-destroyed leaves are discarded. Yet this leaf was placed in a most important location, on the top. Despite its half-eaten condition, this leaf looked so shiny. This leaf had no hesitancy, no inferiority complex. It did not matter that it was "imperfect." It was treated no differently than a "perfect" leaf would have been. There was a deep philosophy in this flower arrangement. We are apt to become attached to what we normally consider the good or perfect things in life. This imperfect leaf teaches us that even dead leaves have a living place.

Our daily lives are continuously challenged by many things. Life is complex and filled with innumerable choices. We need to look into our own lives and understand how to meet the many things which confront us today. Our consumer-oriented society bombards us with a tremendous number of effective advertisements. Department stores and supermarkets have so many similar items; yet each claims to be the best and we must choose one for our individual needs. Often we do not know which is best. We are faced with instant choices and immediate decisions. There are many other changes that could be listed—in fashions, in technology, and in the increasing mechanization so prevalent today. There also have been changes in our morals and many different lifestyles are possible today.

Our way of life is too dualistic: right and wrong, good and bad, this and that. These shallow multiplicities dilute our lives. We have to be ourselves. If we are controlled by our environment, endless frustrations and problems result. One must live his own life. We have to realize that the world in which we live is of our own making. It is by straightening out our own minds that we can become serene and happy. Buddhism is a subjective way of life. Each individual creates his own world. Each individual has a place. Each of us is unique and perfect. Some of us are short, some are tall. Some people are more skilled than others. It does not make any difference. Everyone is the best in this whole world.

I am reminded of a story about a monk named Banzan. One day as Banzan was walking through a market, he overheard a customer say to a butcher, "Give me the best meat that you have." The butcher replied, "All the meat in my store is the best; every piece is the best I have." Upon hearing this, Banzan was enlightened.

The discovery that *each* of us is the best is very important. This holds not only for each individual but also for what is done. Each time we do something is crucial; each moment is of unique importance. Every word we speak and every little thing we do is unique and perfect. A "trivial" thing is the most important thing in the whole world. Buddhism brings this kind of awareness to life. We become aware that a half-eaten leaf is a perfect leaf.

WASH THE DISHES

A novice monk approached the teacher and said, "Please teach me Buddhism." The teacher asked, "Have you eaten?" The novice replied, "Yes." The teacher said, "Then, wash the dishes."

This is a famous dialogue. After eating, it is only natural to wash the dishes and clean up. This way of naturalness is the Buddhist way. When help is needed, go and help naturally— without a sense of obligation or duty. Giver and given are forgotten.

Clouds appear in the sky according to causes and conditions. They move on as they should. Water flows from higher to lower. Man is part of nature. Why do we not live naturally? When our ego appears, there is so much artificiality and pretension. Yes, life is sometimes hard— very hard. But life must be lived. It cannot be escaped. We get sick. We become helpless. That is life. Face reality squarely and don't be defeated; don't be arrogant. When it is hard, endure. Help others and be helped. This is the natural way.

When we do things, however small, do them one hundred percent. We do not make many mistakes in the big things of life. We make mistakes in the little things. Life, after all, is little things put together. Each doing should be done one hundred percent, so that at the end of the day there will be no regret. A Buddhist life is a life of no regret.

To wash your dishes after you have eaten is a common, natural thing. Buddhism is not something special. Live like the wind; live like the water that flows. Do everything sincerely and completely—your life will become perfect. Perfect without any comparisons, for there is no general criterion as such. Each one lives his own true life. This is what the teacher meant when he said, "After eating, wash the dishes."

INDIFFERENCE TO CRITICISM

In general, criticism and abuse are the most common causes of anger and bad feelings between people. How quickly we are upset or angered if others verbally abuse us!

Gautama Buddha never became upset or angry when others criticized him. He remained quite self-possessed in response to even the harshest criticism. Ananda, one of his disciples, once asked him, "Why is it that you can keep calm and not be affected at all by abuse?"

Buddha replied with a parable: "Suppose there is a man who puts filth on a silver tray and offers it to you. Will you take it?" Ananda answered, "If it was filth, I certainly would not take it!" Then the Buddha said, "Well, if you don't take it, who has it?" Ananda replied, "The one who offered it must still have it." "Quite right," the Buddha said, "abuses are like filth. That is why I do not receive them. There is no reason for me to become angry or excited. If you do not receive abuse, you will not become angry at anyone. It is no problem at all. You suffer because you make the abuse your own."

Abuse and criticism are not bad in themselves. You can profit by them if you learn from them by taking a serious look into yourself. If the criticism is true, accept it as fertilizer for growth. If the criticism is false, then it has nothing to do with you. As a matter of fact, great people are often criticized as much as they are praised.

No matter how hard we try, we cannot control the minds of others, and there are always some who will find much in us to criticize. My teacher, Akegarasu, used to remark, "When a ship moves forward it creates a wake. The bigger the ship, the bigger the wake." We cannot avoid stirring up criticism by our actions, however good our intentions. But like a ship which has already moved past its wake, we should leave criticism behind.

EASTER

On Easter all Christians throughout the world celebrate the resurrection of Jesus, the Christ. An individual, Jesus, became the Christ. I don't know if this idea is traditional theology or not, but when Paul Tillich lectured at the University of Chicago many years ago, he said, "Jesus became Christ." This was the first time I had heard such an interpretation. It seems to me that we Buddhists have a similar interpretation. We feel an individual man, Gautama, became Buddha.

Jesus carried the cross up to Calvary. This is very important. Even though he was crucified, he lived up to his true life. He could not be dishonest to himself. Let the rulers of society kill him. In the face of execution he was unafraid. He had something beyond death. Though he died physically, he did not die. He lived all the more by dying. Our life is something like that. There is something worthy in all of us. It can be called the true self, the Buddha, or Christ . . . it doesn't matter. Each of us has something to live up to. Compared to this something, death doesn't matter. Confucius said, "This physical body is lighter than a single hair of the ox." It is life which has weight. We will give up the physical body for this kind of life. If one finds the Way in the morning and dies that same evening . . . life was worthwhile. One should not be afraid to die. One should be afraid of killing one's own true life. Resurrection means the awakening of this true life. This was Christ's greatness. He accepted all conditions and was never defeated by circumstances; he lived his true life. This spirit has provided great inspiration.

The important thing is to discover what we are and be what we are. Assume complete responsibility for yourself. Even if the whole world is against you, what of it? No one can really stop your true life. We have to awaken to this life in ourselves. In Christian terminology this is the resurrection of the Christ in each individual life. Each individual should become a Christ just as Jesus became a Christ. This is how I interpret Easter.

EVERY DAY IS A GOOD DAY

At the entrance to my house there is a scroll written with five Chinese characters. The scroll was written by Ryokan, a Zen monk who lived about three hundred years ago. His calligraphy is beautiful; the meaning is also beautiful. The characters read, "nichi nichi kore ko jitsu." They mean, "Every day is a good day."

Every day is a good day, not a good day as compared to a bad day, but all days are good days; there are no "bad" days. To a city person planning a picnic, rain spoils the day. To a farmer watching his plants, rain is welcome. To the city person the day becomes a "bad" day because his expectations were disappointed. But the day itself is not a bad day. The day is good but the way a person meets the day makes it a bad day or a good day. All days are good days, regardless. We are the ones who make comparisons according to our expectations. We are the ones who turn some days into "bad" days.

It is true that things often do not go right. Home life can particularly be a problem. Between husband and wife there is often more than just disagreement. Through lack of communication real coldness can develop. We are human; we have different feelings. Misunderstandings arise; we make mistakes. We have problems; life means problems. But it is up to us whether we become depressed or not or whether we get angry or not. This is the scroll's teaching.

It is a Japanese custom to decorate the walls with scrolls rather than pictures. Written on the scrolls are typical Buddhist phrases. It is wonderful to have such scrolls to remind us of the teachings. It's a good day but how foolish I am. Why do I complain? Even complaining will not make things better, only worse. To understand that every day is a good day is Buddhism. This is the content of enlightenment. Enlightenment is not something apart from an ordinary day. Enlightenment is to live each day as a good day.

LIFE'S EMPTY SPACES

There is a saying in Buddhism, "When you sit, sit. When you stand, stand. But above all, don't wobble." This means that one should fully concentrate on whatever one is doing. The emphasis is on the *complete* doing of an activity. It is important to know what doing something *completely* means. It means that once you are finished, you should leave it behind and move on to the next thing.

We have to learn how to control our minds so that we can create a mental gap or a void between two activities. This "empty space" keeps us present-centered so that we can concentrate completely on one task and then move on refreshed to the next task. By controlling our minds I do not mean suppression. I mean we should be able to guide our minds. Minds are sneaky. Compared to our bodies, the mind is dishonest. The body does not lie; it can go so far and then takes a rest. The mind does not know when to take a rest; sometimes it keeps going until one becomes mentally ill. It is easier to control our bodies than our minds. We can consciously decide to rest our bodies, and usually we can relax physically. In contrast, our minds are difficult to control and we usually cannot direct it according to our wishes.

Each individual has his own mind and yet one is unable to control it. The mind wanders and all kinds of thoughts uncontrollably enter one's mind. In Buddhism one learns to make one's mind peaceful. By disciplining the mind, selflessness in thought is attained. This is difficult. Selflessness in physical activity is easier. One can become so involved in doing something that one forgets oneself. It is more difficult to stop thinking about something when one wishes to do so. It is habitual for the mind to wander. In fact, some people feel it is a good thing to let the mind wander when doing some routine task. It may seem efficient for example, to be thinking of other things when vacuuming the carpet—but it only *seems* good. Actually, it is better when vacuuming, to just vacuum. Do one thing at a time. Do it completely and when you are finished with it, be done with it completely too.

Worry results from not knowing how to proceed. You can learn from others how to *do* something but you have to learn by yourself how to make a decision. Happiness is not something you obtain. Happiness is when you are actualizing something you want to do. Hard work is happiness if it is a fulfillment of your life. One who is doing something he does not want to do is a most unhappy person. The greatest enjoyment is living a creative life. Decide what you want to do and do it! If it cannot be done, then do something else. Whatever it is, do it completely. Then leave it behind and move on to the next thing.

Between one activity and the next, there should be a space, a vacancy, a cushion. Just as when the body is tired and rests between tasks, so the mind should take a "mental break" and refresh itself. Taking such a break or pause is very healthy. One's mind does not naturally take such a pause. We worry continually and constantly about so many things; it is not surprising that we become mentally fatigued.

My teacher, Rev. Akegarasu, was such a busy person and yet he always had energy. Everyone wondered why he never seemed tired. One time he told me, "You know, many people think I don't get tired. I *do* become tired but I get refreshed quickly. It is very important to pause or make an empty space in the mind. Even half a minute between mental activities is a tremendous rest. If you have these gaps, you don't get fatigued."

We should become more aware of the margins around our activities. The margins should be blank and empty of thoughts; they should not be cluttered by spill-overs from the preceding activity. In *sumie,* Japanese ink painting, the use of empty space is emphasized. This empty space is often just as important as what is actually brushed onto the paper. In the same way that empty spaces are creatively used in *sumie,* we should learn how to create "empty spaces" in our lives.

PACIFY MY MIND

A young monk came to Bodhidharma, the first patriarch of Zen Buddhism, and asked, "My mind is troubled. Please pacify my mind." Bodhidharma said, "Well, bring me that mind." "I cannot bring you my mind!" the monk replied. "There," said Bodhidharma, "it is pacified."

This is a very interesting dialogue. We think we have troubled minds. Actually there is no such thing as a troubled mind. The monk could not bring Bodhidharma that mind; he could only talk about it.

Living is a fascinating process. We are able to smile and able to get upset. Of course, we say smiling is good and being upset is bad. But I don't think that being upset is bad. We are alive—this is why we get upset. Becoming upset is an aspect of life. Although no one is happy about being upset, the trouble is not the being upset but the attachment to being upset—that is the trouble.

We think troubles come from the outside. But really, trouble comes from within ourselves. All life starts from within and goes outward. Of course one might say, "It is the warmth and sunlight from the outside that makes flowers grow." Yet, no matter how much sunlight there is, unless there is life within, nothing will grow. The environment is the stimulation but the real source is within our own lives. Whether smiling or being upset, it is our own doing.

The young monk came to Bodhidharma and said, "Please pacify my troubled mind." However, when Bodhidharma asked, "Bring me that mind," the monk could not do it. It was all within him. No one to blame. If we want to blame, we should blame ourselves. We tend to blame outside things. But when we return to ourselves, the problem will be solved. Our minds will be pacified.

ONE MORE STEP

There is a famous saying, "Climb to the top of a hundred-foot pole, then climb one more step." Anyone can climb up the hundred-foot pole and reach the top. But how can one climb another foot beyond, over the top? This is the puzzling part and also the most important part. After having reached the top one should not become attached to the top; one should not stay there. We become attached to lofty concepts and ideas. Instead, come down to earth and live life as usual. "One step more" does not mean one step up but means to come down. Come down and live an enlightened life in the midst of human troubles.

When we are climbing up the hundred-foot pole, we are very careful. Yes, we can do it by our own efforts—by disciplining ourselves physically and mentally. Many people stay up there saying, "I have done it. This is it!" But the important thing is coming down, down to earth. "Earth" means our everyday life: working, cleaning, cooking, doing chores. When we realize this, then we do all these things in our daily lives— but no longer as victims! We no longer live in a haphazard way. With no attachment to ego, life is at its best. We forget ourselves and put our whole lives into whatever we are doing. The natural self flows out. This is the one step more.

FORTUNE IS MISFORTUNE

I recently visited Plymouth Rock. The Pilgrims came to the new world on the Mayflower. There were 102 people on the boat and two persons died on the way. The Pilgrims landed in a land where no one waited for them and everything was unknown. Nothing was prepared for their comfort; they went through a struggle for survival. The Pilgrims had a purpose of freedom so they were willing to go through the hardships and struggles.

When we consider our lives today, our lives are very comfortable, even more than that, luxurious. We appreciate some things, but our sense of appreciation is so shallow today. Unless we go through trouble and hardships, we really do not experience real appreciation.

In a similar fashion, Enlightenment is difficult to realize when everything is going well. In other words, fortunate people can be very unfortunate as far as religion is concerned. Most of you are fortunate people. You were born into a nice family, brought up with loving care, and never experienced real hunger. Your lives are comfortable and secure. Yet, because of your good fortune, there can be less motivation to deepen your awareness and appreciation of life. The same kind of point is made in the Bible where it says that going to heaven for rich people is as hard as it is for a camel to go through the eye of a needle.

When everything is going well—health is good, plenty to eat, enough money—perhaps we feel we do not need Enlightenment.

However, we need Enlightenment because inevitably we will encounter trouble in life. We will have many problems— be they personal or social, physical or psychological. Having so many problems actually means that we have many occasions to become enlightened. When we get sick, we really appreciate good health. When we do not have much to eat, we really appreciate food. Being fortunate is to be unfortunate and being unfortunate is to be fortunate. We want to be happy, but we do a lot of things that cause unhappiness. We know overeating is a cause of trouble, but when food tastes so good we overeat and thereby invite trouble. In the same way, when things are going too well in our relationships with our spouses or friends, we tend to take things for granted. We do not appreciate other people and create causes for our troubles.

Many times it is only through unfortunate conditions or situations that we realize the value of friendship, kindness, or love. It is ironic that through unfortunate events, we attain a fortunate life. Life is full of such ironic contradictions. It is important to take the time to think about the reality of life. We should take time for self-reflection and re-evaluate our lives. We need to look into our own lives and realize that we really are fortunate, not only in times of good health and plenty, but we are fortunate in every way. All our misfortunes enable us to really appreciate life. Unless we have trouble, we will never appreciate peace of mind. Perhaps this is human nature. We take things for granted and never appreciate things when they are going well. When things go wrong, we become serious and look within. We look deeper into the reality of life and discover real appreciation in life. Real happiness is not what we have, but depends on our attitude and way of appreciation. When we learn that misfortune is fortune, we discover appreciation. Religion is nothing but this way of appreciation.

CONTROL YOUR MIND

Are you able to control your own mind? If you wish to empty your mind, can you? Unless you train, you never can. The mind is yours, but it is hard to control. It acts like a billiard ball rolling around and bouncing off whatever it strikes. Many people in our society are unable to control their own minds. Why do some people become "neurotic"? It is because so many things are constantly on their minds and they are unable to release them. They try to calm down and forget undesirable thoughts, but are completely unable. The businessman is involved with competition and many complex relationships during the day. At night when he leaves his place of business, he is unable to leave his concerns behind. He takes them home with him. Frequently he even takes his worries to bed and is unable to sleep.

Yesterday I had a telephone call from a young man who was involved in a conflict at work. He claimed his fellow workers were jealous of him and extremely spiteful toward him. The situation had reached the point where he could not get a good night's sleep. "What can I do?" he asked. So I told him, "Well, just forget about it. It is all gone. Finished. Why do you become attached to the afternoon's events? It is not a matter of determining right or wrong. Regardless of whether you caused them to get angry or whether others mistreated you, forget about it. When you go to work tomorrow, start a new day. Every day is a new day. Every life is a new life. Don't stay in a new life with the events of yesterday. Tomorrow, act as if nothing happened yesterday; say hello to those fellows. Be kind. Be natural. Don't carry yesterday with you. People may be surprised to see that in spite of yesterday, you don't act spiteful. You can be a clean, fresh person tomorrow. You can control yourself; you cannot control others. Regardless of others, start a fresh new life each day."

Whatever it is, the problem is what we create.

There are reasons to get angry, but we have to remember each day is a new day. Each day should not be started with the defilement of yesterday. We have to be independent of yesterday, independent of others. We are human beings. Yes, sometimes we feel sad or hurt—that is life. We cannot ignore our humanity. But attachment is what makes us miserable. We cannot control society but we can take care of our own minds. It is important to establish ourselves as free and independent persons. Buddhism, it is said, is naturalness. Buddhism is awareness. Buddhism is friendliness. These things we have to learn. We have to discipline ourselves.

In spite of the relative world we live a subjective life. We create our own worlds. I create my world. You create your world. If you are wearing tinted glasses the whole world is tinted. The whole world is your own creation. That is why it is so important to see your own true nature. You will then see the world as natural. Nothing will hinder you; nothing will bother you. A free, independent person—he is a Buddha.

NON-ATTACHMENT

The mind is tricky; often we do not know in what direction it might move. The most unexpected things can happen in one's own life. Even a thoughtful mind can wind up in trouble. Take for instance the teaching of non-attachment. Recently I have come across so much confusion concerning the idea of non-attachment. People know, "I should not become attached to things." However, they are attached to the very idea of non-attachment. This is really the subtle work of the mind!

A man has lost his beloved wife. He thinks of her often and is overwhelmed with sadness. He cries. He says, "I know the teaching of non-attachment. The accident happened and she is gone. I should forget. Why am I crying? Am I a bad Buddhist because I am attached to something that happened in the past? Is crying bad?"

I told him, "You are attached to the idea of non-attachment. Your wife was very dear to you; she meant so much to you. You cannot forget her. She is still with you. Non-attachment is not detachment. When you cry, cry. Crying is not bad. Tears are often beautiful. Your trouble is not that you are attached to your wife, but that you are attached to the idea of non-attachment."

We have to remember that non attachment and detachment are two different things. Life is non-detachable and we are trying to detach ourselves from it. This is the difficulty.

You cannot detach yourself from life. You are living. The world consists of subject and object. When this subject and object become one it is beautiful. When everything is objectified and becomes two—then trouble occurs.

Attachment occurs only in the dichotomized world. When we are one, there is no attachment. Attachment means two. When you dichotomize things into two, then you become a victim and a slave. The true life is oneness and from oneness comes non-attachment. Non-attachment is living one life; there is only oneness, the oneness of all things.

BE YOURSELF

Religions usually center around the idea of salvation, which means to be saved. When one speaks of being saved there must be two factors, one who saves and one who is saved. This is the general concept in most religions. In such religions there is a dualistic approach in which one says petitionary prayers to some external power in order to be saved. The way you are saved is that God saves you. It is believing in a prayer of "Please save me" or "Please help me."

Buddhism has a totally different approach. In Buddhism there is no dichotomy of saver and saved. The term salvation or being saved does not apply in the way of Buddhism. Instead, Buddhism talks of Enlightenment. Enlightenment means to enlighten oneself, to find out that you are you. To become yourself is true "salvation." When you really become yourself, there is fulfillment, realization, and satisfaction. Buddhist teachings all deal with how to become you, yourself. This "you" is a great problem. Who are you? You will not find the answer outside of yourself. You must look into yourself. You can come to the center of yourself and here find and realize your true self. Some people may interpret this as a selfish, self-centered approach.

It does sound egotistical to say the Buddhist way is to realize that "I am I." However, this "I" is not the ego self, it is the true self. Actually, a better way to express this is to say that this "I" is beyond the dualism of ego self and true self.

There are no two "I's." The I that is realized is where the ego self and the true self really become one. It is when all things come from within. There is no regret in such an absolute, subjective way of life. If you are moved by external things, then surely there will be regret. Buddha taught that you must become you. All his teachings center around this finding yourself. By being yourself you truly actualize what you are. You have to look into yourself and be yourself.

When one realizes his true self he will be able to see how others are truly themselves too. This holds not only for other people but for all other things in nature. When I see a pine tree on a cliff, summit, or whatever location, its true self shines forth. The pine tree stands stately as a pine tree against all kinds of wind and weather. I say to the pine tree, "Oh, you stand there under the scorching sun, against the freezing north wind. You are always there, never escaping. You are a courageous pine tree and you give me inspiration and courage." The pine tree becomes my teacher.

In feeling we hug each other and become good friends. So it is with everything else. We all have to be ourselves. By becoming ourselves we realize the oneness of all things. By realizing this state of understanding, there results communication on a higher level of life with other people, pine trees, bamboo, stones, or whatever it is. There is a very sweet and harmonious sharing of life, a oneness, a real hugging of life. Whether it is between people or other things in nature, we become one in a state of true life.

THREE MAJOR TEACHINGS

Buddhism teaches three basic things: Impermanence, Non-self, and Non-attachment. The doctrine of impermanence means that all things are in constant change; all things are continuously becoming. We live a new life each day and each moment. For this reason the Buddha said, "Do not cling." Our life is always fresh. Everything about us—mentally, physically, spiritually—never reaches a stopping point. We are continuously moving on, like a wheel. This is tremendous. We have to be aware. Without this transitoriness our lives would become stagnant and stale.

The second basic teaching is the doctrine of non-self. One should not become attached to the self as if there is an "I" or "You" as a permanent, rigid, important thing. One's life is not an exception from nature. As all things in nature change so one's life itself changes. There is no unchanging, permanent entity called "self." The doctrine of non-self does not mean the denial of individuality. You live a unique, individual life. This uniqueness is very important. Buddhism emphasizes being yourself. There is no person like you in the whole world.

Flowers are flowers, leaves are leaves, roots are roots. Each has its own important function. In buildings—walls, floors, ceilings—each has its own unique place and function. So too with all of us. Each one has his own absolute, unique life to live. Don't imitate others. Only when one lives his own true life is there a true sense of respect for others. This is the true principle of democracy. Be independent and respect each other.

Since the self is always changing, constant self-introspection is necessary. Life is finding oneself and being oneself. Because of non-self, one's life every day is a new life. Discipline and education are important because one does change. One lives a beautiful life every day, without comparing it to others' lives. One's life is good—absolute good.

The first two teachings, Impermanence and Non-self, point to the true way of understanding. That is, to understand the changing world in which we live and to understand that there is no static entity as the self. Due to such understanding, the Buddha taught that the true life is the life of non-attachment. This non-attachment is the third major teaching in Buddhism. When we look into ourselves, we find that we are attached to so many things. We are nothing but bundles of attachments. Such attachments create trouble in our lives. If we are attached to favorable conditions, we become greedy. If we are attached to adverse conditions, we become angry. We are attached to people, to words, to material things, to ideas, to conditions, and furthermore we are attached to ourselves. When we are able to live a life of non-attachment—like the water flowing in the river—there will be no stagnation and no stale conditions. Life will be always fresh and clean.

Buddha taught these basic things: Impermanence, Non-self, and Non-attachment. A serene life is the result of a proper understanding of these three major teachings in Buddhism.

BEARD OR NO BEARD

There is a story about Wakuan, a famous teacher who upon seeing Bodhidharma's picture said, "Why does this Bodhidharma have no beard?"

Bodhidharma brought Zen Buddhism from India to China in the 6th Century. He had a heavy beard and all pictures and drawings of him show this. On the surface, the story about Wakuan makes no sense. Why should Wakuan while looking at a picture of Bodhidharma with a deep, heavy beard say, "Why does he have no beard?" At first I did not understand this story. Now I understand what Wakuan is trying to say.

We conceptualize many things. Through our conceptualizations we have expectations. When someone asks us about Bodhidharma, we say, "Bodhidharma? Oh, yes—that bearded man!" When one says, "He is a Buddhist," we have a certain image of a Buddhist. The same with a Christian; the label "Christian" carries a certain image. We conceptualize and form attachments to these words. We do this with other people, things, and events. We create certain concepts in our minds, have set ideas about things and make judgments based on these concepts.

Perhaps Wakuan was trying to destroy the strong conceptualization of "Bodhidharma has a heavy beard." He was trying to break the duality of "beard or no beard." We humans like to make things rigid and definite: this is so, that is not so. This is red and that is green. We are habituated to concepts that compare things. He is a good man. He is a bad man. "Oh, blacks, they are bad, beware." Some blacks are bad, some are good; likewise for whites and every other race. There are no rigidly set things. The Buddhist point is: all things do change; all things are constantly moving on. However, we want to keep things as they are. We conceptualize things, and if they do not turn out according to our conceptualizations we are disappointed.

Conceptualizing keeps our minds in a status quo. We need to break this conceptualizing and bring freshness into our lives. This is why Wakuan says, "Why does this Bodhidharma have no beard?" He wants us to break the over-intellectualization, the rigid, definite ideas. We have to go beyond beard or no beard. Do not conceptualize, generalize, or become attached to such thoughts. This is the point of the story.

If only we could live like young children. A young child is naive; he does not conceptualize. He does not depend on the past but has a sensitive attitude toward each moment. Give him a little candy and he is overjoyed! The whole world enjoys the candy with this child.

As we grow up we conceptualize and judge things by past experience and kill the precious present moment. We make the present a dying present. We lose the sensitivity and freshness of each moment. If we live like a child making every moment lively, we can really enjoy life.

When you laugh, laugh heartily. When you cry, cry. Living every moment is the way of Buddhism. Each moment is a precious moment. Live each day as a new, fresh day. That is the point of the story about Wakuan. It is trying to break dualistic thinking by presenting the exact opposite. You have to understand that true life is always fresh and always beautiful. This is what Wakuan meant when he said, "Why does this Bodhidharma have no beard?"

ESTABLISH YOUR CENTER

You must establish your center in order to make life truly meaningful. It is only when you have not found your center that you become disturbed and look to external things for help. In our lives we are dependent upon external things. If a businessman were asked, "What is the center of your life?" he might respond, "My center is making money." Someone else might respond, "I'm not interested in making money; I am interested in love, or friendship, or understanding." However, what if these things are not forthcoming?

We expect other people to behave in a predictable way. When our expectations are not met, we become upset. Our anger is a reaction to the environment. Greed is also a reaction to the environment. When things work out nicely we expect this to continue and our ego demands more and more. Unless we are aware, good environmental conditions are as much of a pitfall as misfortune.

You have anger and greed because there is no established center in your life. There is no center from which all your activities, words, and thoughts flow. If you do have such a center, you will not be disturbed in life. Establishing this center is a way to enlighten yourself. From this center life must express itself; it is a matter of life or death. If life does not continuously gush forth, it will die. Life cannot be other than itself. A plant, if it cannot grow, will die. Water must flow—if not, it stagnates. There is something in life from which life moves on—we can call it the center. Where is your center? Or are you content to just exist? Find out what you want. This is the very reason Siddartha, although destined to become a king, went searching to find a free, enlightened life. He found something more than being a king. He became a truth-seeker and established his own life—not a king's life, but his life.

This is the teaching of the Buddha. Each individual has unique, absolute value; it is not necessary to follow the crowd or compare yourself with others. You should establish your center and be yourself. One does this not by depending on external things but by looking deep within. When you find yourself, life becomes meaningful and all things open up for you.

IMPERMANENCE

The first principle of Buddhism is the doctrine of Impermanence. Impermanence means that nothing is stationary, static, unchanging. All things are moving, dynamic, becoming. Life is a continuous becoming. All things in life are constantly becoming. Perhaps it is better to say "changing" since if we say "becoming," then we think, "becoming what?"

Buddhism teaches us to understand that impermanence is the true nature of all things and people. Everything is continuously changing, continuously becoming, continuously new. Through ignorance we become attached to persons, acts, and words. If one thinks he is better than others, he is apt to become upset because others do not live up to his expectations of them. On the other hand, if one feels that others are better than himself he is apt to suffer from an inferiority complex. This kind of behavior represents our ordinary way of life. We always fall into these pits of life. It is hard to adjust ourselves to the changing environment.

If we understand the changing nature of reality, then we will not cling to so many things. Our lives are basically attachment. It is easy to become attached to so many things: possessions, words, deeds, thoughts, and "isms": communism, capitalism, stoicism, asceticism. As soon as something becomes an ism there is attachment. When it becomes an ism, it is dead, it is stale. While water is constantly flowing, it is pure and fresh. When it stops moving, it becomes stagnant. It is the same with our lives. We living beings must live and to live means to change. Often we do not flow with change. Instead, we become attached to our thoughts. Then our thoughts become isms and the isms begin to compete and conflict with each other.

All our difficulties result from attachment. There are no such things as: this is good and that is bad; this is right and that is wrong. Everything is relative and depends upon situations and conditions. Situations change. Monetary, social, political, individual factors—such conditions change. If one becomes attached to the bad, indeed it becomes worse. Even good things, once attachment is formed, become bad. If we are attached to the fact that we have given, we become greedy and expect thanks or something in return. When we give we should simply give with a sincere heart. When it is done, it is done. Everything should be done like this. We should do things sincerely and whole-heartedly. The "doing" is the happiness. The essence of life is not exchange. The true life simply moves forward with sincerity coming from within.

Buddhism points to the reality of constant change. One can make his life ever fresh and ever interesting. However, attachment kills this fresh, new life. If one really understands the reality of this universe which includes all things and all lives, then one's life becomes really beautiful and fresh. This is why Impermanence is the first principle of Buddhism.

MEDITATION

Meditation means serenity in life. Many people think that meditation is to sit cross-legged. That is only a small part of meditation. Nor is just being quiet necessarily serenity. For instance, when a person gets angry and decides not to talk, externally it may seem quiet but internally it is not quiet at all.

True serenity is dynamic, like a generator revolving at a speed of thousands of revolutions per minute—very stable, very quiet, but very dynamic.

In our life the serenity of meditation is not simple quietude, but a real strength that comes deep from within. When it is expressed as quietness it is deep and serene. When it is expressed as action it is dynamic and harmonious. To maintain this serenity of mind is central to our lives, for it enables us to see clearly the truth of life.

If a pail of water is still and serene the surface will reflect the moon. But if the pail is unsteady and the surface is not still there will be no reflection. Our minds, when we are serene, are able to reflect the truth about life and all things. When we are upset we cannot see clearly the truth about ourselves or others. When our minds are disturbed, as in anger or disgust, even a small stone on the road seems to frustrate us. We kick it in anger whereas the stone is faultless, and we are only reflecting our own distorted mind.

A calm mind makes the greatest difference in the way we live. The right kind of serenity is essential to our lives, and this we call meditation.

CONTINUOUS CHANGE

A basic teaching in Buddhism is: *mu jo,* which means "not always the same." In other words, "All things are in constant change, constant becoming." To know Buddhism is to understand this continuous change of all things. Life is *mu jo.* To understand *mu jo* is to understand the truth of life. This idea is not unique to Buddhism. Heraclitus, the Greek philosopher, said that all things are like fire. Fire is a constant transformation and because of this burning and changing, fire has energy.

Although it is in the nature of things to change, our ego wants to keep things the same. We want to keep life as it is. We desire constancy. We fear change. Most of all we do not want to die. However, when we are born it has already been decided that we will die. Birth and death are not two things. Death is included in life. Life means death. Each day and each moment we continuously experience this life-and-death process. Each moment our previous life dies and a new life is born. Each day we live a new life. We never live the same life twice. When we plunge our hands into a moving stream, we cannot place our hands in the same water twice.

Although life and death cannot be wiped out because it is a continuous process, if one understands and lives according to this process of life-and-death, that in itself is complete extinction of life-as-such and death-as-such. Duality is totally transcended. Life and death are one continuous, simultaneous process. Disappearing is appearing; appearing already means disappearing.

Without death there is no birth. Without destruction there is no creation. Buddha's greatest discovery was to realize the simultaneous nature of creation and destruction. This is truth; this is reality. Our lives are no different from all things in nature. Summer follows spring. After summer, autumn comes. It is a continuous process. Buds blossom into flowers, flowers turn into seeds, and seeds become new plants. If we really understand this reality, it will show in how we live.

Today will not be repeated tomorrow. Tomorrow is a new day. Today happens *only once.* Just as a flower blooms for only a short period, one's life is only once. A flower is beautiful because it blooms and dies. We must appreciate the flower here and now. Plastic flowers lack this beauty and we can have only a shallow appreciation of them. The world is beautiful *because* it changes. We can appreciate all stages in the process of change. Even though according to certain values, one stage could be considered more attractive than another, once we realize the reality of "once-ness," all stages are beautiful. Only once! This is *mu jo.*

To understand *mu jo* is to be able to appreciate, to respect, and to live life fully. If we understand this, we are able to take whatever comes. It is this understanding which creates peace of mind. Peace is when things change naturally. Water flows peacefully. Fire burns peacefully. Life moves on peacefully. Peace is not stable or constant. Peace is dynamic. If you conceive of peace as a static state, then that is not peace. Peace of mind is to know things as they are. Things are *mu jo*; reality is *mu jo*. If you live in *mu jo*, life is beautiful. Every moment is precious. This is the basic Buddhist teaching of impermanence or continuous change.

TRANSCENDING MEANS AND ENDS

Buddhism emphasizes transcending a means-end kind of thinking. You have to go beyond the attitude of being motivated to act only in order to get something. If you study Buddhism only in order to gain enlightenment, this is a wrong attitude. True reality is only when seeker and sought are one. The very doing is the realization of the Buddha's way. When you wash dishes, wash dishes—nothing else. When you sleep, you sleep—nothing else. When you do something, put your whole life into it. When you say something, mean it. Do not pay lip service, make pretensions, or behave artificially in order to achieve results.

Buddha Dharma refers to things as they are. When a flower blooms, that is Buddha Dharma. When you take a walk, take a walk. Don't imitate, don't follow. Singleness in thought, in saying, in doing—this is Buddha Dharma. A flower blooms without regard to blame or praise. When water fills a tank and reaches the top it overflows. No ifs or buts. But life in our modern society is very troublesome because there are so many ifs and buts. Buddhism points to a life where there are no ifs or buts. Do not seek things. The means is the end in itself. To transcend duality is the Buddha Dharma itself. The more you realize this the deeper you will understand the reality of life in all things. This is the Buddhist teaching of transcending means and ends.

BUDDHA'S FACE

Once a philosopher came before Gautama Buddha and challenged him, "Teach me Buddhism—but I do not want a verbal answer and I do not want silence for an answer." This person was famous and well-learned, so it was a great challenge. Many disciples were gathered around the Buddha and they were anxious to see how the Buddha would deal with this challenger. It is written that the Buddha simply changed seats and looked at the philosopher. The philosopher saw the Buddha's face and responded, "Thank you, most compassionate Buddha, I understand." And he bowed in deepest respect.

The face is said to be the window of the mind. We all have to take responsibility for our faces. The face is honest. It shows what we have inside. If we are buoyant, have gusto for life—it shows. If we are troubled and hateful—it shows. All Buddha statues show a bright, august, wise expression—not a smile but just a trace of a smile. Man may cover his body, but not his face.

So the visitor thought he would challenge the Buddha and win. Instead, he received a great lesson from the Buddha. The truth cannot be explained. A verbal answer is not an answer when it comes to the truth. Silence is not adequate either. Life must be communicated, beyond words and silence, from mind to mind. The Buddha conveyed to the philosopher something intuitive, something transcendental. The teaching is not something explained in books, spoken of in lectures, or given as answers to questions.

The truth is conveyed not by action and not by words—but by life itself—and by life it is understood. Only life can understand life. The philosopher in the story must have been at that point in his life where he was able to realize this teaching instantly. The true teaching, true life, is something communicated directly between two persons. In this way, the teaching has been handed down from teacher to student. The teaching is not contained in words or any other formality. We have untold appreciation for the teacher who has shown us something beyond words. This is the Buddhist way of teaching—experience, not words.

RIGHT UNDERSTANDING

We must have right understanding about ourselves and about others. Others means one's family, friends, society, and all the things that one deals with every day. If one sees a rope lying on the road in the evening and thinks that it is a snake and becomes afraid—that is an illusion or a misunderstanding. On a bright day no one would see a rope as a snake. We must have the bright light of wisdom in our lives so that we can see things as they really are.

Most domestic troubles are based on a lack of understanding by wife, husband, or children. Many of us make misjudgments about others by overestimating or underestimating them. Not having right understanding we often expect certain things, and if our expectations are not fulfilled we are angry or disappointed. However, we do not become angry at the misbehavior of a small child when we understand that child as he is—a small child who does not yet understand life. Likewise, if a stranger comes along and insults us for no apparent reason, we become angry. If we later find out that the stranger was an insane person our anger and resentment cease, because we now understand him as insane.

We can transcend many difficulties by accepting things through right understanding. The trouble is that we have the tendency to see only our own view and we neglect to see or understand others. This lack of understanding creates much suffering, not only in personal relationships but also in national and international relations.

We must have a correct understanding of all things; it is especially important to understand oneself. How many of us really understand our own selves? Without having right understanding of oneself, how can one attain true happiness?

Buddha taught, "First, know yourself." Socrates spent his whole life on the knowing of self. My teacher, Rev. Haya Akegarasu, said that the theme of his life's study was himself. To seek truth means to seek the truth of oneself. Yesterday's self is not today's self; today's self will not be tomorrow's self. Each day is a new and different day. Thus, we truly cannot judge anyone or anything as if it were the same each day because all things are different from day to day.

Our tendency to see others according to our own point of view is dangerous. Thieves see only a world of crime, and a selfish person only a world of greed. Too many of us see things through our own glasses which are colored by our prejudices and preconceptions. How difficult it is to have right understanding! Yet how many tragedies occur because of wrong understanding. The right understanding of Buddha's teachings of 2,500 years ago in India is vitally important as we apply those teachings to our American life here in the Twentieth Century.

husband was gone, she was so lonely. Although she had no prior health trouble, she suddenly died. It often happens that when one's life companion passes away, the other person does not live too long. This aged couple was one such example.

When we hear about the death of someone, we are saddened. It also makes us think more deeply; we realize we are subject to death too, regardless of age or health. Suppose you were sentenced to death next week by your doctor. You would think about life. Unless we think and remind ourselves, our lives become monotonous and our lives will just pass us by. Each day will be just another day. However, when a friend passes away, particularly a young person, the reality of death hits close to home.

A very good friend and a charter member of our temple moved to California many years ago. About a month ago he called me and said, "Well, Sensei, I have cancer. The doctor says that it is terminal. The first thing I thought about was you and I had to call you." Yesterday somehow I thought of him and called to see how he was doing. He spoke in such a small voice and said, "Please remember me. I think my end is coming soon." I couldn't help but shed tears. We spoke for a while and said good-bye. It was such a sad good-bye. This is the reality of life and it always comes back to me and it comes back to you.

I am reminded of Buddha's teaching, *"Ichigo, ichie."* *Ichigo* means "one life" and *ichie* means "meets only once." So the teaching means that we meet only once in a lifetime.

EVERY DAY IS THE LAST DAY

A group of students were visiting the temple recently and I talked to them about Buddhist teachings. Afterwards there were questions and one student asked what the Buddhist way of life was. I said that it was to live each day most beautifully and most meaningfully. Then he asked what happens when we die. I explained that Buddha did not talk about such unknowable things as what happens after death. Philosophers may speculate about such things, but Buddha always said that the most important thing is here and now, how you live the present moment. This is important because all things are subject to change. Life is transitory; we should live each day the best we can. Then if anything happens there is no regret. Each day is complete in itself. Live every day sincerely because each day is the last day.

The reality of this truth really hit me because last week several friends passed away. One was only 20 years old. He was a straight "A" student in his second year of college. His father was very proud of him and expected a great future for his son. The son developed liver trouble and was sick only about a week before he died. Death came unexpectedly and the father took it very hard. His sadness was so deep. There were no words to comfort him. However, this is the reality of life. Time is the only thing that will heal his wounded heart. Another person, one of our older members, was 90 years of age. Her husband also died about six months ago. After her

That is to say, every time is the last time. I meet you today but who knows if we are able to meet next Sunday. So, Buddha said, "Every day is the last day." We should live accordingly.

BIOGRAPHY

Rev. Gyomay Masao Kubose was born in 1905 in San Francisco, California. He received his primary and secondary education in Hiroshima, Japan. In 1922, he returned to the United States. In 1935 he graduated from the University of California at Berkeley, majoring in philosophy. He then went to Japan and became a disciple of the late Rev. Haya Akegarasu with whom he studied in Japan for five years, traveling with his teacher on lecture tours throughout Japan, Korea and China. Rev. Kubose was ordained as a Shinshu minister and given the Dharma name "Gyomay," which means "bright dawn." Rev. Kubose returned to the United States in 1941 and spent the war years in relocation camps.

In 1944 Rev. Kubose relocated to Chicago and founded the Buddhist Temple of Chicago and has been its spiritual leader ever since. The Buddhist Temple of Chicago was founded as an independent religious organization with no administrative ties to a higher headquarters of any other Buddhist sect. Its founding purpose was to make Buddhism available to all Americans by presenting the teachings in Western terminology. In connection with the Temple he established the American Buddhist Association in 1955.

In 1966 Rev. Kubose returned to Japan to study Buddhism at Otani University in Kyoto and earned his Masters Degree. During this time he also studied and practiced Zen Buddhism. Upon his return to the States in 1969, he established a meditation group and also the Buddhist Educational Center as part of the Buddhist Temple of Chicago. He teaches at the Center in addition to lecturing widely here and abroad. He has been cited many times for his work in the field of brotherhood and community relations. In 1970 he received the World Buddhist Mission Cultural Award. Throughout his life, Rev. Kubose has emphasized and taught non-sectarian Buddha Dharma for all.

BOOKS BY GYOMAY M. KUBOSE

Everyday Suchness

Zen Koans

Heart of the Great Wisdom Sutra
(translation and commentary)

American Buddhism

Tan Butsu Ge
(translation and commentary)

Fundamental Spirit of Buddhism
(translation)